THE DARWEN COUNTY HISTORY SERIES

A History of
WARWICKSHIRE

Richard Blome's 'Mapp of Warwickshire with its Hundreds', 1673

THE DARWEN COUNTY HISTORY SERIES

A History of
WARWICKSHIRE

Terry Slater

Cartography by Jean Dowling
Marginal illustrations by Tim Grogan

Phillimore

1997

Published by
PHILLIMORE & CO. LTD.
Shopwyke Manor Barn, Chichester, West Sussex

First published 1981
Revised edition 1997

© Terry Slater, 1997

ISBN 0 85033 991 X

Printed and bound in Great Britain by
BUTLER & TANNER LTD.
Frome, Somerset

To Diane, David, Sarah and Daniel
for their friendship

Contents

List of Illustrations

List of Colour Plates

Acknowledgements

The courtesy of the following is gratefully acknowledged for permission to publish illustrations: Mr. G. Dowling, A.R.P. S., for plates V, VI, VII and VIII; Mr. R. C. Swift, A.I.I.P., A.R.P. S., 107; Brian Hobley, F.S.A. and Coventry Museum, 16; Warwick County Record Office, 131; Shakespeare Birthplace Trust Record Office and Lord Willoughby de Broke, 77; Birmingham Reference Library, Local Studies Department, 32, 33, 36, 42, 43, 49, 64, 65, 71, 102, 103, 104, 113, 124, 125, 145, 151; University of Cambridge Aerial Photograph Collection, 34, 76 copyright reserved; Arnold Baker, F.S.A. and the National Monument Record, 10, 11, 19, 93; School of Geography, University of Birmingham, 51, 55, 56, 70, 72, 92, 108, 109, 119, 123, 130, 133, 134, 141, 143, 144, 148. Figure 97 is based on a plan in the Warwick County Record Office. The remaining plates are derived from the author's photographs. The front dust jacket is provided courtesy of Royal Leamington Spa Art Gallery and Museum (Warwick District Council Museum Service). I am grateful to Mr. G. Dowling, A.R.P. S. and Mr. S. Restorick for photographs of the maps, engravings and historical photographs used for the illustrations.

Preface

There are many excellent histories of the county of Warwickshire as well as comprehensive and voluminous chronicles of the two great cities within its ancient bounds: indeed, the first modern county history of any shire was Sir William Dugdale's impressive *Antiquities of Warwickshire Illustrated*, published in 1656. However, there are few concise volumes in print which survey the whole chronological spectrum from the prehistoric period to the 20th century and which provide a summary of recent historical research. In writing such a book it is, of course, impossible to do more than introduce the long and complex history of the millions of people who have lived, and worked, and died in this part of Midland England and to suggest ways in which those inhabitants have left their imprint on the landscape through the centuries. In Warwickshire that problem is compounded by having a great medieval city and two important industrial conurbations within its boundary. Separate chapters provide more detail for medieval Coventry and for Birmingham in the 18th and 19th centuries, but elsewhere, if they were not to take over the book, Coventry and Birmingham have had to play second fiddle to the rest of the shire. The treatment is broadly chronological, but in order that the history should not become a disjointed summary of dates, places and people, particular topics have been selected to give some coherence. There are unavoidable omissions of facts, details and whole subjects, but it is hoped that some of these are at least introduced in the maps, illustrations and marginal drawings which are an important part of this series of histories. The book is concerned with the county before the reorganisation of local government in 1974; it therefore includes those areas anciently in Gloucestershire and Worcestershire until the Victorian rationalisation of county boundaries. It is anachronistic to talk of Warwickshire at all for the period before about A.D. 1000, but its use is more convenient than using some alternative term for the region discussed.

1 *Sir William Dugdale, Warwickshire historian*

I remain grateful to those people who assisted in the completion of the first edition of this book. As always, the archivists, librarians and staff of the Warwick County Record Office, the Shakespeare Birthplace Trust Record Office, and the Birmingham Reference Library were unfailingly courteous and helpful. Professor Peter Daniels has allowed me to use the facilities of the School of Geography, University of Birmingham in producing the revised text and illustrations for this edition. I am especially grateful to the late Jean Dowling who drew the fair copies of most of the maps and to Kevin Burkhill

2 *Warwickshire County Council arms*

15

3 *Coventry city arms*

for additional cartographic work, to Tim Grogan who prepared the marginal drawings, to Ron Swift and Geoff Dowling for photographic work, and to Claire Fothergill and Lynn Ford who shared the typing of the revised text between them. I have gained immeasurably from conversations with academic colleagues and former students and from their written works. The late Professor Harry Thorpe introduced me to the delights of the landscape history of the county, and I have learnt much from Brian Roberts, Christopher Dyer, James Bond, Della Hooke, Keith Lilley, Dick Holt, Nigel Baker, Carl Chinn, Maurice Beresford, Lindsay Proudfoot, Margaret Gelling, Peter Jarvis, Graham Webster, and Eric Grant; errors of fact remain my responsibility, not theirs. This revised edition has seen the text reorganised to fit a new format and extended to take account of new archaeological discoveries and historical research over the past 15 years. The most substantial addition is a section on 17th-century religion and on the Civil War and I acknowledge my debt to the writings of Ann Hughes and Philip Tennant in compiling this chapter.

A new edition allows for a new dedication; the Barge family are Warwickshire born and bred and for most of the past twenty years have extended their friendship and hospitality to this particular eccentric academic. I thank them for it most warmly.

1

Introducing the County

Warwickshire is part of the Midland heart of England and contains within its bounds a great deal of the English people's soul of history and literature. Places such as Kenilworth, Warwick, and Stratford-upon-Avon deservedly attract thousands of visitors each year, both from Britain and overseas, who seek to savour something of that history in today's countryside, townscape and buildings. The county presents two faces to those visitors. Two-thirds of it is predominantly rural; a prosperous, well-cultivated countryside of brick and timbered farms, thatched cottages, neat villages and ordered fields. The remaining third encompasses a similarly prosperous landscape, but one of industry, commerce and suburban housing, since the great urban areas of Coventry and Birmingham are contained within the bounds of the old shire.

4 *Garrick's Shake-speare theatre, 1769*

Coventry was one of the largest and most prosperous cities of medieval England, so much so that it became a county in its own right in 1451. In the 19th century it expanded rapidly again, firstly on the basis of silk-ribbon weaving and watchmaking, then the development of light engineering and the making of bicycles. In the present century motor-cycle and motor-car manufacture came to the fore, and, until recently, Coventry, for the second time in its history, was considered one of the most prosperous towns in England. Birmingham got off to a later start, growing rapidly through the 16th and 17th centuries though its variety of metal-manufacturing trades. By the end of the 18th century it had overtaken Coventry as the largest town in the county, and a century later it had attained its present position as the second city of England in terms of its population. Today, Coventry and Birmingham form part of the County of the West Midlands, carved out of the north-west part of Warwickshire in 1974, but the links between these two cities and the surrounding countryside remain strong. Rural dwellers work and shop in the city centres; city dwellers use the countryside for recreation and fresh air.

The County Boundary

The bounds of Warwickshire are for the most part man-made. Only to the south-east does the Jurassic limestone escarpment of the Cotswold Hills form a prominent physical divide with Oxfordshire. The north-east boundary

17

5 *George   Eliot's
birthplace,   Arbury,
Nuneaton*

with Leicestershire runs along the ancient Roman highway of Watling Street for mile after mile. To the west a prehistoric ridgeway rises from the Avon at Evesham up on to the Birmingham plateau west of Alcester, providing extensive views into Worcestershire, but to the north-west and south-west there is little to differentiate the countryside of Warwickshire from that of neighbouring Staffordshire, Worcestershire, and Gloucestershire. Indeed, the medieval shire boundary to the south-west was once extremely complex with islands of one county surrounded by the land of others. This complexity derived from inter-mingled Anglo-Saxon estates so that it was landowners, especially ecclesiastical landowners, rather than landscape which determined where the bounds should run.

Geology, Topography and Drainage

The river Avon and its tributaries, the Sowe, Leam and Stour, drain most of the southern half of the county and provide the focus for early settlement and communications. The light gravelly soils of the Avon valley have been continuously farmed since the Neolithic period. Successive waves of settlers moved in from the Severn valley to the south-west and over the low ridges from the Welland valley to the north-east, and the Cherwell to the south-east. The evidence of their hut-circles and farmsteads, superimposed one upon the other, shows up today on the aerial photographs of archaeologists. Between the Avon and the Cotswolds the Roman Fosse Way runs parallel to river and hills along a low Liassic limestone ridge. This road continues to serve the rich agricultural Lower Lias claylands of the south of Warwickshire which were so intensively cultivated in the medieval period as to become known as the Feldon, or field-land. These corn fields were converted to pastures for sheep and cattle in the 15th and 16th centuries. Villages tumbled beneath the grass and fortunes were made by landowners who then converted their profits into mansions and parks. Today the fields are back under the plough again, often for the first time for 400 years, and the Feldon is again a corn-growing field land.

The south-eastern fringe of Warwickshire is marked by the steep escarpment of Jurassic limestone which forms the Cotswolds. The heights of Edge Hill reach up to 700 ft. and the ramparts of Iron-Age hill forts and medieval castles guard the top of the scarp whilst across the fields towards Kineton was fought the major Civil War battle in 1642. There are gaps in the scarp though, the headwaters of the Cherwell allowed the Oxford canal and, more recently, the M42 motorway to cross the Cotswolds into Oxfordshire, whilst the Fosse Way slips south into Gloucestershire where the headwaters of Stour and Evenlode have sapped the height of the hills at Moreton-in-Marsh. The slopes of the scarp have provided floriferous sheep pasture for two thousand years or more.

North of the Avon there is a rather different countryside; more wooded, pastoral, and with scattered hamlets and isolated, often moated, farmsteads. It is a gentle, plateau country of Mercian mudstones and sandstones dissected by fast-flowing streams—the Tame, Rea, Cole, and Blythe flowing north to join the river Trent in Staffordshire, and the Arrow and Alne flowing southwards to join the Avon below Bidford. In Anglo-Saxon times this was a more sparsely populated countryside, quite heavily wooded and with extensive areas of heath and common. This 'Arden' region thus became an area of opportunity between the 11th and the 16th centuries where families could enclose a farm, build a house, use the products of the woodland and the power of the tumbling streams to improve their lot and that of their children. Country houses such as Umberslade, Baddesley Clinton, and Packwood were built from profits accumulated by such entrepreneurs, to be followed in their turn by the detached houses and double garages of those who have found their fortune in 20th-century Birmingham. This distinction between Arden and Feldon regions in Warwickshire is noted by the Tudor historian, John Leland, who wrote in about 1540 'that the ground in Arden is muche enclosyd, plentifull

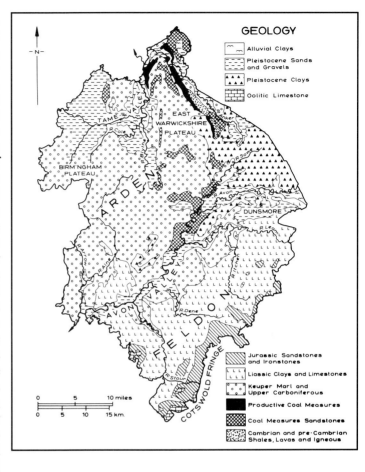

6 *The geology of Warwickshire*

of gres ... and woode, but no great plenty of corne. The other part of Warwykshire that lyeth ... to the southe, is for the muste part champion, somewhat barren of woode, but very plentifull of corn'.

A third countryside makes up the north-east of the county, the East Warwickshire plateau. Sandstones again, but Coal Measures sandstones, so in this region there is also hard quartzite and a narrow outcrop of coal running in an arc from Tamworth to the outskirts of Coventry. From at least Roman times the coal-seams have made this an industrial region. Roman potteries and tile kilns are known at Mancetter and Hartshill; textiles and leather crafts followed in the medieval towns of the Anker valley on the eastern side of the plateau, and in Coventry, while the coal was mined on a successively greater scale as century followed century. Canals were dug to take it off to power the machinery of factories in Birmingham and London, and railways followed where canal had led. However, excepting Nuneaton, the mining villages remained just that—villages set in a pleasant rolling countryside, because the narrowness of the coal outcrop limited development until the beginning of this century.

7 Ann Hathaway's cottage, Shottery

The eastern corner of the county provides another distinctive small region. Here, the headwaters of the river Avon, and its tributary the Leam divide around Dunsmore, a small plateau of lacustrine clays topped with infertile porous gravels. This was poor heathland in medieval times, shared by neighbouring communities but settled only by the poor and dispossessed.

Warwickshire is a tamed landscape then; there are no wild parts untouched by people, and in the grimmer corners of Birmingham, Nuneaton, and Coventry, generations of humanity have made a very unlovely landscape from their exploitation of nature, and of their fellow men and women. However, much of the countryside remains very beautiful. There is the natural beauty of willows and meadowland beside the gently-flowing Avon, the golds and browns of oak and beech in an Arden autumn, or breathtaking views across Midland England from the top of Hatton canal locks or from Edge Hill. And there are generations of man-made beauty: country houses such as time-mellowed Compton Wynyates, nestling in its combe, or Warwick Castle perched dramatically on its sandstone cliff; villages such as Warmington below the Cotswold edge; earthworks such as those that mark the deserted village of Wormleighton; small timbered market towns like Henley-in-Arden, and fine modern townscapes such as the Cadbury's Bournville suburb and Birmingham's redesigned and pedestrian-friendly city centre. The unravelling of the contributions given to and taken away from that landscape by each generation in turn provides the theme of this history.

2

Prehistoric Peoples and Roman Colonisation before A.D. 410

Until quite recently the region that was to become Warwickshire was regarded by archaeologists as comparatively less interesting than the chalk downlands of Wessex or the limestone uplands of the Cotswolds. The Midland countryside was thought to have been thickly forested. Settlements in pre-historic times were considered to have been few and far between, and certainly there were not the numerous and often spectacular earthworks and monuments of more-favoured southern counties. Since 1940, this picture of Warwickshire before the Roman invasion has gradually been revised, and since 1960 has been changed quite radically by evidence gathered using new scientific techniques. Some of these revisions apply not just to the local countryside of Warwickshire, but to our whole picture of prehistoric society and settlement in England. It is now established, for example, that many places are far older than previously assumed and that some prehistoric events took place over a much longer time span. Different prehistoric cultures, previously thought to result from 'invasions' of culturally superior Continental groups, are now seen as changing slowly from one culture to another, often with long periods of co-existence in both time and space. The boundary lines between the Late Stone-Age, Neolithic, peoples, the Bronze Age, and the Iron Age have thus become extended periods of gradual change, rather than sharp breaks.

The Stone Age

In the West Midlands the greatest change has been in the realisation that the prehistoric countryside was not a primeval forest with a widely-scattered population, but, possibly from 3000 B.C., was as intensively cultivated and densely settled as it was in the 13th century. Even before this, Palaeolithic, or Old Stone Age, people were already living in the upper Avon valley around Coventry where their stone axes have been found, fashioned from the local quartzite, and another group are known from Little Alne, north of Alcester. Mesolithic, Middle Stone-Age, people are known to have dwelt along the Avon valley and in the Tame-Blythe basin. They used flint tools and possibly shifted their homes from site to site, cultivating small areas and hunting and fishing.

8 *Neolithic knife and arrowhead from Welles-bourne*

21

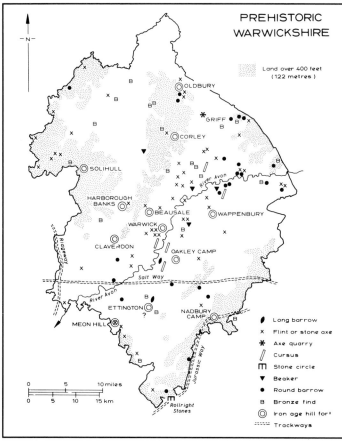

9 *Prehistoric Warwick-shire*

By about 3,000 B.C. the first agricultural revolution had reached Warwickshire and the culturally more advanced Neolithic peoples had become well-established. They used bone and wood as well as stone for their tools; they used local clays to make pottery; they lived in more settled communities farming the land and clearing extensive areas of woodland for their crops; they built long barrows, to inter their dead, and the earliest-known henge monuments to worship their gods. Only three or four long barrows are known in Warwickshire, all in the middle Avon valley between Warwick and Stratford. There is a small cursus in the same area near Thelsford, and others at Barford and Wellesbourne, while the only surviving henge monument, the Rollright Stones, stands on the Cotswold border with Oxfordshire at the southern tip of the shire. However, excepting the Rollright Stones, most Neolithic monuments survive only as crop marks visible on aerial photographs and it is likely that in this intensively cultivated area there were other such henges, which have been removed by 4,000 years of plough cultivation. The main finds of Neolithic pottery have been slightly farther north between Warwick and Coventry, but this reflects the pattern of archaeological excavation as much as anything. Much pottery has been found in recent years around the sandstone knoll on which the modern town of Warwick stands, and it is possible that this was a centre of some importance with a ring-ditch fortification. Large numbers of stone axes and hammers of Neolithic age have been found over a wide area of Warwickshire. The majority were of local origin since, as well as the quartzite ridge in the north-east of the county, quartzite and flint pebbles are plentiful in the Boulder Clay on the sandstone plateau of Arden and in the river-valley gravels. A quarry at Griff, near Nuneaton, is thought to be the source of one large group of stone axes found in the Sowe and upper Avon valleys; while others in the region came from the Graig Lwyd quarry in North Wales and from Langdale in Cumbria, so long-distance trading must have been already underway.

However, it was changes in agriculture that brought about the greatest alterations in the landscape. The gradual change from mixed farming-hunting communities shifting from place to place, to more settled groups living

10 . *Multi-period cropmarks at West Grafton. Aerial photography has revealed a large number of prehistoric settlement sites on the gravel soils of the Avon valley. This site at West Grafton shows trackways, field boundaries, hut circles and rectangular enclosures*

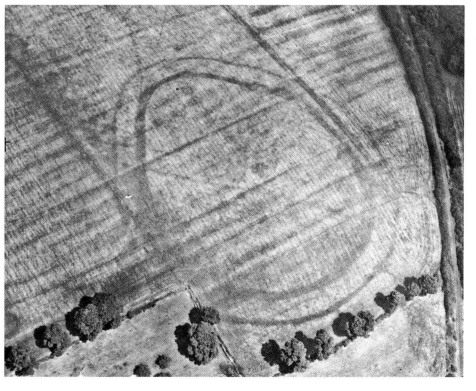

11 *Iron-Age hillfort at Ettington. Many hillforts survive as upstanding earthworks, but this one at Ettington, in the intensively cultivated Feldon, has been ploughed out and survives only as a cropmark.*

entirely by their farming skills meant that more people could be fed from a given area of land. Consequently, population grew and more land was then taken into cultivation until a new equilibrium between people and their environment was reached. In Warwickshire, this 'first agricultural revolution' began on the fertile, easily-cultivated gravel soils of the Avon valley and the Tame-Blythe basin. Once these areas were being fully utilised, settlers moved out to the more difficult soils of the Feldon where again patches of lighter soils within the claylands were the first to be exploited. They moved, too, up on to the sandstone soils of the Arden plateau. One result of the clearance of woodland for Neolithic farms was that large quantities of soil were washed from hillsides into streams and rivers to be deposited lower down the valley as alluvium. It is the considerable depth of alluvial deposits, about Alcester for example, which give the clue to the area of countryside that must have been under cultivation.

The Bronze Age

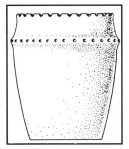

1 2 *B r o n z e - A g e cremation urn from Ryton-on-Dunsmore*

The most significant relict of the Bronze Age in Warwickshire is the remains of some thirty round barrows, the circular tumps in which the Bronze-Age peoples interred their dead, or at least their dead leaders. Most of them are now ploughed flat, but a few, such as the pair at Burton Hastings, survive as upstanding monuments. In total, relatively little Bronze-Age material has been either found or excavated in Warwickshire. Characteristic pottery 'Beakers' are known from Baginton, near Coventry and urns, used to hold the cremated ashes of the dead, have been found in barrows at Brandon, east of Coventry, and Oldbury, near Mancetter, while a small cremation cemetery has been excavated at Ryton-on-Dunsmore. Most of the pottery finds come from the Sowe and Upper Avon valley areas. Bronzes include a dagger found near Rugby, four swords found at Meriden, and small spearheads from near Fillongley and Leamington. A bronze chisel was unearthed during the excavations at Barford, near Warwick, which proved to be a complex farming site occupied from the Neolithic through to the Iron Age.

A characteristic site of Bronze-Age date is the so-called 'burnt mound'. These are especially numerous in the headwaters of streams on the Birmingham plateau. They consist of mounds of pebbles and charcoal. The pebbles have been heated and rapidly cooled causing them to crack eventually. Archaeologists have interpreted them either as debris from cooking, using heated stones, so-called 'pot boilers'; or as a prehistoric steam bath, or sauna, the hot stones being plunged into water to produce the steam.

The Iron Age

From the sixth and seventh century B.C., iron tools and weapons began to be used, and iron currency bars such as those found at Meon Hill fort were used for trading. Good quality pottery, often wheel-turned, was characteristic, and Iron-Age people seem to have lived in small communities, perhaps extended families or groups of two or three families. Their farms consisted of large round dwellings made of a circle of timber poles with low wattle-and-daub walls and a thatched roof. Examples have been excavated at Barford and Wasperton among others. Smaller huts were used as barns and byres, and pits were used for storing grain and burning rubbish. These farms were surrounded by a ditch, probably with a palisade fence or hedge, and there were small enclosed fields beyond. On the gravel soils of the Avon valley and in the Tame-Blythe basin, these farmsteads occupied almost all the cultivable land and there was little waste or uncultivated countryside. Intensive arable farming demands a complementary pastoral economy so that cattle or sheep can be turned onto the fields during the winter months to manure the soil. It seems probable that in the summer cattle, sheep and pigs were driven to the pastures in the less-densely populated areas of the plateau county of Arden and East Warwickshire and to the Cotswold fringe.

Though living in small groups the Iron-Age people were organised into larger tribal groupings whose leader possibly occupied the hill-forts which are the most notable relics of the period in the present landscape. There are 12 such forts in Warwickshire, but it is unlikely that all were occupied continuously. Some, with a single low embankment, might be cattle enclosures, while others might have been constructed hastily in response to the Roman invasion. However, others were built in areas which had long been a focus of occupation such as the triple ditch system in Priory Park, Warwick, or the massive embankment that encloses Wappenbury fort, near Leamington. Another enigmatic earthwork is the linear embankment near Tanworth-in-Arden, known as Hob's Ditch Causeway, which might be part of an Iron-Age tribal boundary since it can be traced over a distance of some three miles.

13 *Romano-British pin from Tiddington*

The currency bars found at Meon Hill and at Nadbury on the Edge Hill escarpment indicate trading activity, as do the Dobunnic coins of the later Iron-Age period and the organisation of pottery production at particular centres. Trade and the effective political organisation of the tribe required effective communications and certainly by Iron-Age times there was a complex network of trackways across Warwickshire. The Jurassic Way, a group of linked tracks of great antiquity, ran along the south-east boundary of the county, on the Cotswold scarp, while part of another long-distance route running east-west crossed the Avon at Stratford and left Warwickshire near Wormleighton. This route was probably used, among other things, to take salt from Droitwich to the Avon valley people and on to the East Midlands. A north-south route also crossed the Avon near Stratford, linking the Cotswolds to the Clent Hills, perhaps continuing to the Severn at Bewdley and on to Wales. Another more local route ran parallel to the Avon on its north side, and there were undoubtedly other such trackways in the northern half of the county.

The Romano-British period

The conquest of Britain by the Roman armies proceeded in definite phases. Within four years of landing in Kent in A.D. 43 they had subdued opposition

14 *Samian pottery fragment*

15 *The Fosse Way near Brinklow. The great military road of the Fosse Way bisects southern Warwickshire. It began as an early frontier line across Britain. The modern road diverts through Brinklow where a medieval castle was built across the Fosse*

as far as a temporary frontier along the Jurassic scarplands. From this frontier, marked by the construction of the Fosse Way road, they pushed progressively north-westwards into the West Midlands before the uprising of A.D. 60, led by Boudicca in East Anglia, forced a retreat to old forts with retrenchment and reorganisation. Conquest then advanced again, and by c.A.D.75 the military had evacuated the area of Warwickshire to civilian rule and had moved further north and west. One result of this long period of military activity was that a large number of forts were built in the area that was to become Warwickshire. One group was located on the major roads: Mancetter (*Manduessedum*) and High Cross (*Venonae*) on Watling Street, Chesterton on the Fosse Way, and south of Alcester on Ryknield Street, while there was a very large marching camp at Metchley, in Birmingham, also on Ryknield Street. There are probable forts marking the first advance from the Fosse

Way at Orchard Hill, near Stratford, and at Budbrooke, near Warwick, and a complex cavalry fort of the later, A.D. 60-75, period at the Lunt, near Coventry. The Lunt fort, which has been partly reconstructed, includes a feature so far unique in Britain in the shape of a *gyrus*, a training ring for horses. Elsewhere the rectangular forts were enclosed by a ditch and rampart with timber palisades, corner towers and gateways. Within, a grid of streets gave access to timber barrack blocks, houses for officers, granaries and stabling.

After the advance of the army, the Warwickshire countryside found itself very much a second-class area, and the native Celtic population were allowed to continue farming much of their land. There were none of the great villa estates so characteristic of the Cotswolds a little further to the south, nor of the take-over of land for redistribution to retired soldiers, which occurred around Gloucester and Colchester. There is little evidence either of the wholesale redistribution of land to Roman capitalist entrepreneurs since marketing seems to have developed slowly. In most instances it began around the forts. Traders, who had gathered at the gates to supply the soldiers, stayed behind when they moved on to provide for the needs of travellers on the new paved highways. Thus Chesterton, Mancetter and High Cross, for example, developed into small trading communities strung out along the main roads. They were also the sites of *Mansio* buildings, the guesthouses for imperial messengers travelling the highways. That at *Tripontium* has been excavated. The courtyard building there had a heated room and very fine painted plaster.

16 *Reconstructed gateway at The Lunt Roman fort; the Lunt fort, south of Coventry, was a cavalry barracks and contains a, so far, unique gyrus for training horses. A gate-way, part of the defences, and a granary have been reconstructed as part of a museum project.*

As a small trading settlement Chesterton seems to date only from the mid-third century. The earthwork defences enclosed timber-framed shops lining irregularly laid out streets. A more important place was Alcester, which was probably the largest settlement in Roman Warwickshire, and the only one which was properly a town. There was a small walled town centre and south of this walled area was an extensive grid of roads servicing a major trading complex of workshops and associated housing. Tanning, metal working, and pottery manufacture were all important, and there were large cemeteries on the fringes of the town. Alcester seems to have been a major agricultural market centre and some of its houses were quite richly endowed. Some had a dozen rooms or more, heating, painted plaster and even mosaic floors.

Mancetter was also an important settlement in the midst of an extensive industrial area of potteries which extended up on to the quartzite ridge of Hartshill, near Nuneaton. Some thirty kilns are known in this area producing *mortaria*, or kitchen mixing bowls. Production began in the early second century and men such as Locius Vibius and Minomelus were exporting their wares all over the northern military zone of Britain. The potters customarily

17 *Mortarium potter's stamp from 'The Lunt'*

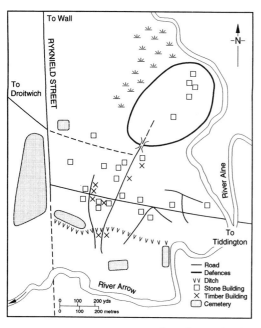

18 *The plan of Roman Alcester*

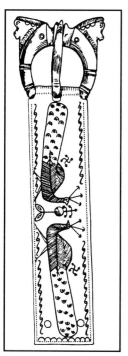

19 *Late Roman bronze buckle from* Tripontium

stamped their names on the rims of these vessels, and 16 such names are known. The coarse pottery from Alcester is distinctive, but was distributed only in the local rural area, as were the grey kitchen wares of the numerous kilns at Wappenbury, near Leamington. There were smaller pottery kilns at Fenny Compton and Perry Barr. Other industries included stone quarrying for the building trade, particularly from the limestone of the Cotswolds, and tile-making. Clay-fired tiles baked in sophisticated kilns were a Roman innovation and were used mainly for roofing and for the hypocaust pillars of house-heating systems and bath-houses. Tile-making needed clay, sand, water and charcoal for fuel, all of which Warwickshire had in profusion. Most of the tile factories line the north side of the Avon valley with known sites at Lapworth, Kenilworth, and south of Nuneaton. Coal from the Warwickshire coalfield, probably mined near Mancetter and Nuneaton, was sent by road to other parts of the Midlands, including the villa at Shakenoak in Oxfordshire, where it was probably used to heat the hypocaust central heating.

Romanised farm buildings are not common in Warwickshire. Less than a score are known from aerial survey, and they have none of the palatial features of the Cotswold villas. They were quite small, rectangular and probably had timber-framed upper floors. Two such farms were excavated at Ashow, near Kenilworth, where part of their field system—small rectangular enclosures—was preserved in woodland. One farm with timber buildings had been rebuilt in the second century with stone footings, and the second consisted of mostly timber buildings with tiled roofs. They were abandoned in the late third or early fourth century, and the farm reverted to woodland. As well as these Romanised farms, many of the earlier British farms in the Avon valley were allowed to continue and no doubt they prospered with new markets for their surplus produce. At Tiddington, near Stratford, quite a large village of such Romano-British farms developed with evidence of iron working as well as agricultural activity. Farming systems were probably mixed, the fertile soils of the river valleys being used for cereal production and livestock being pastured in the woodland and heath areas during the summer as they had during earlier Iron-Age times. The heavier ploughs introduced by the Romans probably led to the extension of cultivation in the more difficult clay soil areas.

The first Roman temple to be found in Warwickshire was excavated in the late 1970s at Grimstock Hill, near Coleshill. It began as a small wooden building, but this was later replaced in stone with a small apse. Later still, an ambulatory was added around the building which was enclosed by a wall. There was a small bath-house nearby, but there was no evidence as to which deity was worshipped there.

The three great paved roads—Watling Street, Ryknield Street, and Fosse Way—constructed in the first century as part of the military conquest of the region, together enclose the area that was to become Warwickshire. These roads must have been impressive features in the landscape. In all but the driest places they were cambered, twenty or thirty feet wide, and with a carefully graded surface of gravel on a foundation of pebbles and large stones. Side ditches drained off storm-water, and the land for several hundred feet on either side was cleared of vegetation so that there was little danger of ambush or surprise attack. The length of Ryknield Street through Sutton Park is a remarkably well-preserved example of such a highway. Later, in more peaceful times, these military highways were supplemented by other roads often almost as well constructed, such as that between Alcester and Stratford, while the older prehistoric trackways continued to be heavily used.

In the period leading up to the withdrawal of the Roman garrisons in A.D. 410 more and more of the defence of the countryside and the coast was put into the hands of Germanic mercenaries from the Continent. In return for their services many were given land and allowed to settle in Britain. There is more evidence that this is what happened in Warwickshire. The earliest evidence of Germanic peoples is found in strategic places such as the important river crossings at Stratford and Bidford-on-Avon, and at Stretton-on-Fosse. In the first instance the Saxon mercenaries seem to have lived quite happily in the same communities as the Romano-British people whom they were protecting since they shared the same cemeteries, but thereafter order began to break down, more and more Saxon people came to settle the fertile lands of Britain, marginal land went out of cultivation and reverted to woodland, and probably population fell drastically as a result of the visitation of plague.

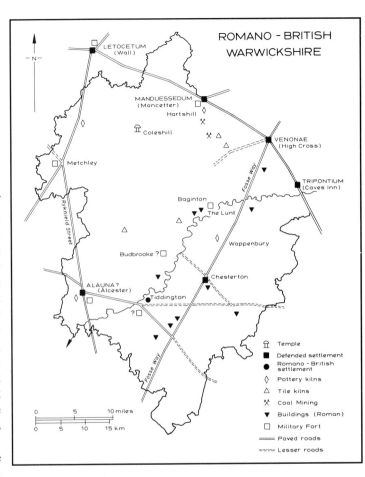

20 *Romano-British Warwickshire*

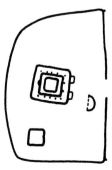

21 *Coleshill Roman temple plan*

3

The Anglo-Saxon Settlement, 410-1066

Pagan Tribes

Warwickshire was settled by two different groups of Germanic peoples. From the east came Anglian colonists travelling via the Wash up the valleys of the rivers Welland and Nene to settle in the upper Avon valley, and coming down the Trent to live in the Tame-Blythe basin, while a second group, the West Saxons, moved northwards from the Thames and Severn valleys into the middle Avon area and south Warwickshire. By the end of the sixth century both Angles and Saxons were an important element in the population, and their main settlements are recognised from cemeteries. They were still pagan and the earliest groups cremated their dead. Cremation cemeteries are known at Baginton, Tiddington, and Bidford in the Avon valley, at Marston, near the Fosse Way, and at Churchover on Watling Street. A little later burial began to replace cremation, and since people were buried with personal ornaments and weapons we know a little more about this group. There are important pagan burials at Longbridge and Emscote, near Warwick, at Wasperton, at Alveston, at Bidford-on-Avon and at Stretton-on-Fosse. The Bidford group were buried with distinctive saucer-brooches characteristic of the West Saxons, while at Alveston, Longbridge and Emscote the highly decorated square-headed brooches of the Anglians have been excavated. There were also iron spear-heads, knives, swords and shield bosses, and beads, pins and other jewellery. Most of these cemeteries were small, representing only a few households who were perhaps the military overlords of the local peasant population.

Once the light of the historical record begins to illuminate the scene, Warwickshire emerges divided between two kingdoms. North and east Warwickshire was part of the territory of the South Mercians, while south-west Warwickshire was part of the kingdom of Hwicce. Smaller tribal groupings are known within each kingdom, mostly based on the river valleys. Thus in South Mercia a group living in the Tame-Blythe valleys took their name, *Tomsaetan*, from the Tame, while in the Hwiccan kingdom a group called the *Stoppingas* occupied the Arrow-Alne valleys, and perhaps the area around Stratford. The Mercian kingdom grew to become one of the largest and most important in Britain in the eighth and ninth centuries. It absorbed surrounding kingdoms, including the Hwicce, whose kings became subject to

22 *Square-headed brooch from Stratford*

30

Mercian lordship in the time of Penda, the last heathen ruler of Mercia.

The early Church

After Penda's death in 654, the new king was converted to Christianity and the first Mercian bishop was appointed. St Chad was consecrated bishop in 669 and built a small church near Lichfield, making this the centre of his see. Ten years later the Hwicce were given their own bishop who established his cathedral at Worcester. The ancient diocesan boundary between the two sees gives the best indication we have of the divide between the South Mercian and Hwiccan peoples since the Church tried to make its dioceses coincide with the political realities of the age. The boundary cuts Warwickshire into two unequal parts. The county south and west of a line from Tanworth-in-Arden to Warwick, Lighthorne, Kineton and Tysoe was in Worcester diocese and therefore part of the Hwiccan kingdom; the remainder, including Birmingham and Coventry, was in Lichfield diocese and Mercia.

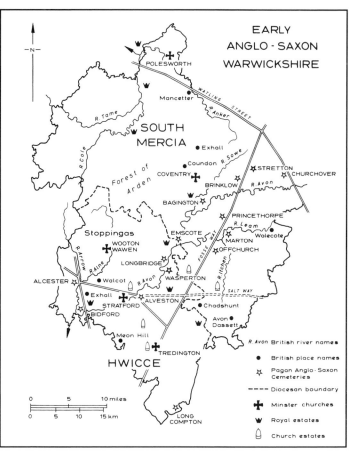

23 *Early Anglo-Saxon Warwickshire*

There is relatively little direct evidence for the work of the Church in Anglo-Saxon Warwickshire, but it must have been much like elsewhere in lowland England. Priests ministered to the people from minster churches, normally small monastic communities serving very large areas and supported by their own estates. Such minsters are documented at Coventry, Polesworth, Stratford-on-Avon and Wootton Wawen between the eighth and early 11th centuries, but there were probably others at places like Coleshill, Warwick and Southam. Some of these early churches were built of wood, but from the 10th century stone began to be used. Nonetheless, only the church at Wootton Wawen retains any substantial masonry from this period, in the shape of its central tower, and part of the nave.

In the ninth century the ideal among the clergy of living in monastic communities declined and, though there was a reversal in the 10th century, by the early 11th century the secular clergy were in the majority and had become more closely tied to the barons and nobles. Most newly-founded churches in this period owed their existence to a landowner building a private estate chapel, and it was these private churches which were to be the basis of

24 *Bronze saucer brooch from Bidford*

the system of parish churches which emerged in the 12th century. To the landowners these churches were just one more source of income, and the priests who served them were just one more vassal who owed them allegiance. It was quite proper, therefore, that Werefrith, Bishop of Worcester, should lease some of the lands belonging to Stratford minster to a thegn in 872, while priests were listed in Domesday as among the tenants of the manor.

The conversion to Christianity was not a simple event in a single year. It is easy to forget that missionary activity continued through to the 11th century and easy to forget, too, that the Church maintained a tenuous toehold through from the late-Roman period. Despite the increasing dominance of pagan Anglo-Saxon settlements, Romano-British people continued to live in the West Midlands probably to inter-marry with the newcomers, and certainly to maintain some of their traditional institutions, including their Christian religion. Place-names give the clue to some of these survivals. The two places called Exhall, for example, the one near Coventry, the other close to Alcester, indicate possible sites of Celtic, rather than Saxon, churches, since the first part of the name is derived from the Celtic *ecles*, meaning a church, and the Celtic term is in turn borrowed from the Latin *ecclesia*. Most river names in Warwickshire are also Celtic, including the Anker, Avon, Leam, Sowe, Cole and Tame, while a few other settlements have names which indicate they were inhabited by Celtic people—the two Walcots for example (meaning cottages of the Welsh), Coundon, near Coventry, Chadshunt, and Avon Dasset. Mancetter derives from the Roman name for the Watling Street station, and suggests the survival of British people there, too. Place-names also commemorate some of the old Germanic gods of the first Anglo-Saxon settlers. The village of Tysoe, nestling at the foot of Edge Hill, derives from *Tiw*, the god of war, while Weoley, in south-east Birmingham, shows the presence of a heathen temple. At Tysoe the villagers had cut a great horse in the turf on the hillside showing the reddish soil below, in similar fashion to the more famous White Horse on the Berkshire Downs at Uffington.

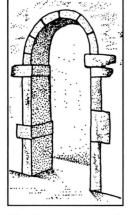

25 *Saxon   arch,
Wootton Wawen church*

Place names

The earliest English settlements in Warwickshire are probably those with topographical names like Radbourn, meaning 'red stream'—ford names as at Bidford, and river names like the villages of Arrow and Alne. But the most common names are those which end with the elements -ton and -ley. The suffix -ton means farm or village, and is most frequent in the south and east parts of the country, while -ley means 'wood' or 'woodland clearing' and is more common in the north and west. This area was the later one called Arden and the -ley place-names show that settlers found considerable areas of wood and pasture here, including much that had re-colonised areas cultivated in prehistoric and Roman times. The first parts of many Warwickshire settlement names refer to early owners or leaders of groups. Birmingham, for example, means 'village, or meadow, of *Beorma's* people';

I *Arden countryside and Maxstoke Priory. Warwickshire's gentle pastoral countryside is well exemplified in this corner of Arden. Maxstoke has a fine moated castle, built in 1346, and the ruins of an Augustinian Priory. The gatehouses and crossing tower of the priory church survive.*

II *The Fosse Way at Princethorpe. This view looks north-east across Dunsmore Heath. The river Leam is in the foreground and the Roman Fosse Way bisects the picture. Wappenbury Wood to the left is a Forestry Commission plantation. The hamlet of Princethorpe developed around a road junction. Princethorpe Priory (centre) was begun in 1832 for French nuns. It is dominated by a huge church built by P.P. Pugin in 1901.*

III *St John the Baptist, Berkswell; the Norman chancel of this exceptional village church is unaltered and has a crypt beneath. There is a lovely late-medieval porch. The churchyard cross (1850) stands on a medieval base and, just to the south-east, is the spring which gives name to the place.*

IV *St Giles, Chesterton. This stark, rather lonely church is mostly early 14th-century; the crenellations date from c.1600. It contains fine monuments of the 16th and 17th centuries to the Peyto family whose grand mansion, demolished c.1802, stood close by.*

Billesley, near Stratford, was *Bill's* clearing or wood; Berkswell was the spring of *Bercul*; and Polesworth, *Poll's* enclosure. One of the more important persons possibly referred to in a place-name was Werburgh, either the saint-daughter of King Wulfhere of Mercia or the wife of King Ceolred. Werburgh forms the first element in Warwick, which can be interpreted as 'Werburgh's trading place'. Warwick possibly began as an eighth-century market on the border between Hwicce and South Mercia and under royal protection or sponsorship.

Mercia reached the height of its power in the eighth century during the kingship of Offa. He reformed the coinage, introducing the silver penny, constructed along the Welsh border the massive earthwork dyke which still bears his name, and consorted as an equal with European leaders such as Charlemagne. Offa had two principal palaces, one in London and the other at Tamworth, which had been a royal residence as early as 691. The palace probably stood on a rectangular platform in the centre of the present town, and the parish church, St Editha's, possibly began as the chapel of this palace. A defensive dyke enclosed an area around the palace and beside the river a sophisticated horizontal water-mill of this period has been found preserved in the waterlogged ground.

26 *South Mercian 'sceatta' coin of King Aethalbald*

The Danes and the Burhs

After Offa's death in 796, Mercian power began to wane, and from 850 a new group of settlers made their presence felt in Warwickshire: the Danes. Danish raiders first entered the Thames estuary in 835, and by 868 the Anglo-Saxon Chronicle records the presence of a great Danish host at Nottingham. In 874 a large part of the Mercian kingdom was ceded to them and, after King Alfred's treaty with the Danish leader, Guthrum, in 886, Watling Street became the established boundary between the 'Danelaw' to the east and the remnant of Mercia to the west. In the early 10th century a combined army from Mercia and Wessex inflicted a crushing defeat on the Danish army near Wednesfield in south Staffordshire, giving the Mercians time to reorganise their defences. This was largely undertaken by Aethelflaed, Lady of the Mercians', widow of King Ethelred, and sister of King Edward of Wessex. The new military strategy was based on a system of fortified towns, or *burhs*, a method already being successfully used by both Wessex and the Danelaw to defend their territory. Between 912 and 918 at least ten such *burhs* were built, two of them in Warwickshire. In 913 the 'lady of the Mercians, went with all the Mercians to Tamworth and built the *burh* there in the early summer' and in 916 'in the early autumn, that at Warwick'. The *burh* defences at Tamworth consisted of a timber-reinforced earthen embankment with an exterior ditch and timber gateways. The people of the surrounding countryside were responsible for the defence of the *burh*, and to facilitate this the owners of rural estates were given plots of land within the *burh* to build houses for their retainers, while in many *burhs* the streets were laid out on a regular grid plan. This was possibly so in Warwick. A

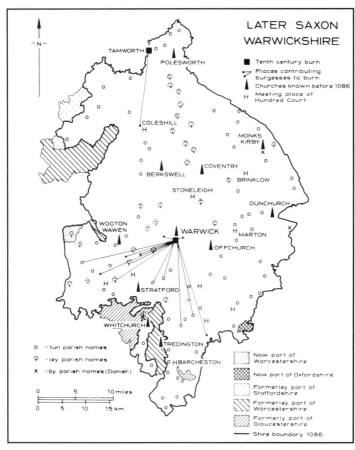

27 *Later   Saxon*
Warwickshire

market encouraged trading while the minting of coinage was limited to the new *burhs* and they became responsible for the administration of the surrounding countryside. Aethelflaed died at Tamworth in 918 and was buried in Gloucester abbey church.

Relatively few Danes settled on the Warwickshire side of Watling Street, judging from the place-name evidence. The ending -by, 'a village or homestead', as at Monks Kirby and Willoughby, indicates Danish influences, but these names also contain English prefixes. Similarly, Scandinavian personal names (Copsi, Kalfry and Thorleifr) are combined with the English -ton in Copston, Cawston and Thurlaston, suggesting that a few Danish overlords had taken over English settlements at a late stage.

Fighting between the Danes and the English erupted again at the beginning of the 11th century, and in 1016 the Danish army invaded Mercia 'slaying and burning whatever was in their path'. At Warwick they burned the nunnery which then stood on the present site of St Nicholas's church, and many a village was left a smoking ruin. It was at this time that the administration of Mercian England was reorganised and Warwickshire first came into being. These periodic episodes of violence, however, were not the sum history of the centuries between Rome and William the Conqueror. Of far more significance was the gradual expansion of cultivation, the growth of population, and the extension of settlement. In the early part of the period, scattered farmsteads rather than nucleated villages seem to have been the typical form of settlement, even in the well-cultivated valley lands of the Avon and Tame. Probably by the 10th century, however, and especially in south Warwickshire, settlements had expanded sufficiently to occupy most of the land that could be cultivated. Thereafter, the majority of the manors in this area were reorganised with a central village settlement whose occupants farmed the land communally in two or three great fields of inter-mingled acre-strips. Some 10th-century land charters show that this was certainly being done around Stratford, at Alveston and Bishopton. Barley, rye and beans were grown there, while at Luddington two teams of oxen and 100 sheep are noted.

4

Warwickshire in Domesday Book, 1066-1086

In 1066, William, Duke of Normandy, made good his claim to the English throne by his defeat of Harold and an English army at Battle, near Hastings. Harold was killed, and William, after securing London, moved quickly to consolidate his Conquest. Norman sheriffs were appointed to the shires, royal castles were hastily constructed and given to Duke William's followers. The Normans came not as settlers, as had the Angles, Saxons and Danes, but as overlords, as tax-collectors and as builders of castles, abbeys and manors. The impact of the Conquest upon the common farming folk and upon the landscape was, therefore, comparatively much less, except in those areas such as Yorkshire and Staffordshire, where resistance was encountered. Here villages were burnt and the land left empty, sometimes for many years, and Domesday Book demonstrates that even by 1086 these regions had not recovered.

In Warwickshire resistance was minimal and the English Lord, Turchil of Warwick, did not involve himself in the fighting. Having secured southern England, and having been crowned king, William marched northward in 1068 to counter strong anti-Norman movements centring on York. His campaign began with the raising of large motte and bailey castles at Warwick and Nottingham. Warwick's castle was perched on the edge of the sandstone bluff on which the town was built, overlooking the Avon crossing. Four houses had to be destroyed to make way for it, and the town's oldest church, All Saints, was enclosed within the bailey palisade. The great earthen motte still survives, mistakenly christened Aethelflaeda's mound in the belief that it was the 10th-century *burh*.

Domesday Estates

At Gloucester, in 1085, William, in consultation with his counsellors 'sent men all over England to each shire to find out what, or how much, each landholder held in land and livestock, and what it was worth'. The information obtained was collated at Winchester, checked, corrected and partially abridged, and then written out in a single great volume—Domesday Book. This massive undertaking, unique in medieval Europe, was completed within a year, and its unprecedentedly full information provides a major source for historical study.

28 *Medieval knight*

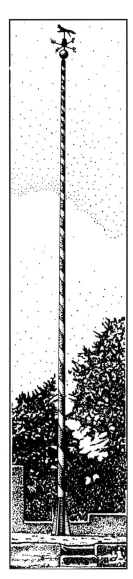

29 *Welford maypole*

The Warwickshire part of the survey records some three hundred places within the shire, which was divided for local administration among 10 hundreds—a much more complex pattern than the four great hundreds of later medieval times. The land of Warwickshire was held by 45 overlords of whom the most important were Robert, Count of Meulan, and Turchil of Warwick, one of only two English barons to retain his lands as late as 1086. Two years later, however, Henry de Beaumont, brother of the count, who had been given the constableship of Warwick castle in 1068, was created Earl of Warwick by William II and to support his title many of the estates of Turchil were granted to him. Soon afterwards he acquired his brother's estates to make up the great honour which gave the earldom its political importance. The king held comparatively little land in Warwickshire directly in demesne. The most important royal estate was Brailes in the southern tip of the county which contained 46 hides and was valued at £55. A hundred villein families lived in the several settlements of the manor with 46 ploughs between them to till the fields. There were a further 30 bordars tilling their own lands enclosed from the waste, and 13 slaves worked the demesne farm. A mill, meadowland and extensive woodland, probably mostly many miles to the north, around Tanworth-in-Arden which was part of the manor, added further to the value. The Bishops of Chester, Worcester, Bayeux and Coutances held land in Warwickshire. The Bishop of Worcester's was the most significant estate and was centred on the valuable Avon valley lands around Stratford-upon-Avon. Of the six abbeys and priories that held estates in the shire, Coventry had the most extensive and valuable estates because of Earl Leofric's generous endowments before the Conquest. They included Southam, Bishops Itchington, Priors Hardwick, and Wasperton.

Farming Regions

The record of agricultural activity, population, woodland and manorial values in Domesday Book reveals strong regional contrasts in Warwickshire. There are three main regions trending south-west to north-east through the county and generally there is a diminution of population density and agricultural activity from south to north. The Feldon, the south-eastern portion of the shire, had been almost entirely cleared of woodland and was intensively cultivated. In this region the plough-teams are generally recorded as equal to the plough lands available for tilling. The number of plough teams per vill is at its greatest in this Feldon region. Most of the settlements were probably already nucleated villages of the kind familiar today, and the surrounding land was cultivated in open-field strip holdings. Alongside the streams lay the all-important and very valuable meadowlands of each community, providing hay and early pasture for livestock. The same streams were dammed to provide power for the manorial mill, another valuable attribute of many estates. The Stour, Leam and Itchen provided the main locations; for example, there were no less than four mills at Honington, on the Stour, together with 40 acres of meadowland, but more typical perhaps was Barcheston, where two manors between them had 22 acres of meadow and a small mill valued at 100 pence. Recorded population in this region is between 10 and 15 per square mile, which means that actual densities probably ranged between forty and sixty per square mile, since only household heads are recorded.

The second region contains the Avon valley and its northern tributary streams. The middle Avon terrace belt between Warwick and Bidford was as prosperous, as densely peopled, and as intensively cultivated as the Feldon region. In the upper Avon valley there were valuable manors, especially around Coventry and Monks Kirby, but soils were more variable and so generally population, plough teams and values were rather lower than in the Feldon. The settlements in the Anker valley around Nuneaton extend this region northwards, while in the south west the valleys of the Arrow and Alne are closely linked with the lower Avon, but the populaton density and values are similar to the northern half of the region. In the middle Avon, between Bidford and Warwick, there was little woodland, population densities of nine to twelve recorded adults per square mile, and a rough equivalence between plough teams and plough lands. There was extensive meadow beside the Avon and many valuable mills such as that of Milverton, near Warwick, which rendered 50 shillings. Complementary to these larger mills were renders of eels, the only mention of fisheries in Warwickshire. The mill at Wasperton

30 *Watermill at the Grange, Bidford-on-Avon. Most manors possessed a watermill by 1086 and the miller was an important member of the village community. The mills were rebuilt several times over until the 19th century but their sites remain unchanged*

yielded 20 shillings and 1,000 eels. In the Arrow-Alne valleys, the upper Avon and the Anker valley there was much more woodland recorded, population densities were between six and eight per square mile, and many more settlements had land that could still be brought into cultivation since plough lands sometimes exceeded plough teams. A typical settlement was Arrow, near Alcester, where there were seven plough lands, but only six ploughs; the families of eight villeins and 10 bordars made up the population; there was a mill worth 6s. 8d., 30 acres of meadow, and woodland a league long and two furlongs wide. The mill was worth £4 to the Bishop of Bayeux in 1086.

In sharp contrast to all this was the third region enclosing the north-west of the county. This upland country of the Birmingham and East Warwickshire plateaux and the Tame-Blythe streams which drain it was much poorer. The density of settlement was very low, there were few villages, population densities were between two and four families per square mile, there were few plough teams, few mills, little meadowland, and a great deal of woodland. Generally, the region was one where there was scope for considerable development with great under-utilisation of resources. The most important settlements were in the Blythe valley and included Hampton-in-Arden, Coleshill, and Kingsbury. Birmingham was an undistinguished village in the Rea valley, somewhat overshadowed by the more prosperous manor of Aston, and its entry in Domesday is typical for this region. There was land for six ploughs, but only three plough teams were used; there were the families of five villeins and four bordars; woodland half a league by two furlongs, no mill, no meadow, and a total value of only 20 shillings.

31 *Burton Dassett post mill*

The Church

Following the Conquest, Norman bishops and priests replaced English predecessors almost as rapidly as Norman lords replaced Saxon, though Wulstan, the Saxon Bishop of Worcester, who was to be canonised saint following his death in 1095, was allowed to retain his office because of his loyalty to the new king. In 1086, Domesday records 63 places in Warwickshire as having priests, rather fewer than in some other counties, though five manors had two, Stoneleigh, Upton, Kingsbury, Monks Kirby, and Long Itchington, suggesting that these places possibly had minsters. The majority of the priests were attached to the early-settled manors of the Feldon, and in the valleys of the Avon, Arrow and Alne and the Tame-Blythe basin.

The new Norman lords began to rebuild many of their manorial churches on a grander scale and in stone. Some of this building work still survives. Probably the best is St John the Baptist, at Berkswell, where the chancel is a complete Norman survival, beautifully built in red sandstone ashlar. It seems likely that Berkswell was a centre of religious activity considerably earlier than normally reckoned. There is an unusual octagonal crypt below the church which seems to have been built for pilgrims to venerate a relic. The powerful spring, *wielle*, which gives name to the village issues south-

32 *The font at St Peter and St Paul, Coleshill. One of several fine Norman fonts in Warwickshire, this font has a richly carved Crucifixion with scroll patterns on each side of Anglo-Saxon derivation*

33 *The crypt at St John the Baptist, Berkswell. This unusual village church has a late 12th-century crypt leading from an octagonal space which might be derived from an earlier Anglo-Saxon church*

east of the church into a stone-walled, 16ft.-square tank which perhaps began as an open-air baptistry. Other fine Norman stonework is found in the chancel at Beaudesert; the solid, round piers of the south arcade at Butler's Marston; the doorway of St Nicholas, Kenilworth (perhaps removed from the Priory at the Dissolution) and the fine carving of the angel tympanum in the north doorway of Halford, and on the font at Coleshill.

34 *Norman doorway at Kenilworth church*

The Towns and Castles

The only town recorded in Warwickshire was the shire town, which was clearly a large and flourishing borough. Its houses were divided almost equally between the king and his barons. There were 113 houses in the king's lordship, and 112 divided among 27 other lords. There were also 19 free burgesses and beyond the bounds of the borough there were a further 100 bordars 'with their gardens'. The town probably had a total population of between 1,500 and 2,000. The borough was surrounded by a ditch dug at much the same time as the castle was being constructed, and the main streets were gated to the north, east and west. Already the town had expanded considerably beyond the bounds of the 10th-century *burh* and, by 1086, it is probable that the Earl of Warwick had already laid out the great rectangular market place, to take some of the pressure off the crowded town centre streets and ensure the orderly growth of the town.

It is possible that Coventry, too, was already a substantial town by 1086, though Domesday gives no hint of this since there is only a typical rural entry under the lands of Countess Godiva. However, it is thought that some important towns were omitted from Domesday Book for separate treatment, and Coventry might be one of these. Its important Benedictine Abbey had been founded in 1043 by Earl Leofric and Countess Godiva, and it may be that the great triangular market place at the west end of the new monastic church dates from this time. By 1102 the centre of the episcopal see had been removed to Coventry. Archbishop Lanfranc enforced a rule that cathedrals should be moved from villages to towns. At first, the bishop had removed from Lichfield, then only a village, to Chester, but he then returned

35 *Brinklow castle and town. The great motte and bailey castle at Brinklow was possibly built by the Count of Meulan soon after the Conquest to control the Fosse Way. Later, it became the hundred meeting place and a small town was planted at the castle gate.* (Cambridge University collection: copyright reserved)

to the West Midlands, to Coventry, which by implication was, therefore, a town. The discovery of a substantial early defensive ditch enclosing part of the town south of the river Sherborne strengthens these possibilities.

Tamworth is another town that remains unrecorded in Domesday, in this instance presumably because it was divided between Staffordshire and Warwickshire and was neglected by the Commissioners for both shires. It was probably still a place of some significance and strategic importance since a motte and bailey castle was constructed beside the Tame river crossing on the southern flank of the borough.

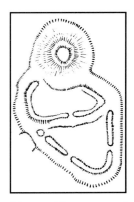

36 *Brinklow motte and bailey castle*

The motte and bailey castle was a Norman innovation. It consisted of a great circular steep-sided mound of earth—the motte—on the top of which a timber tower was erected, and an oval enclosure surrounded by a bank and ditch to one side of the motte which provided room for kitchens, barns and a more spacious hall. The motte at Warwick still survives at the west end of the castle, while the size of the bailey is marked out by the later stone walls and towers built by successive Earls of Warwick. Tamworth castle was built at the same time as Warwick, again in one corner of the Anglo-Saxon *burh*. A third castle of the Conquest period is Brinklow, astride the Fosse Way in east Warwickshire. Brinklow is much more evocative of Norman times since it was subsequently abandoned and is now a grassy earthwork. The motte is about 40ft. high and about 60ft. across the top, while the enormous bailey (400ft. x 500ft.) was the largest in Warwickshire. It is divided across the middle and it is possible that, as the military significance of the place declined, the garrison was reduced and in order properly to man the defences a shorter palisade became necessary. Many of the new Norman lords built smaller motte and bailey castles when they came to Warwickshire to take possession of their estates and began to collect rents and services from possibly recalcitrant tenants. There are good surviving examples at Seckington in the extreme north, which was held by the Count of Meulan; at Brailes, where a raised platform takes the place of the bailey, which was part of the estates of the Earl of Warwick; and at Studley, held by William de Corbucion.

5

The Middle Ages, 1085-1485

Medieval Open-Field Farming

The people of medieval Warwickshire farmed their lands in a number of different ways. In the south and east, and in the Avon valley some kind of open-field system was used over most of the agricultural land of the township. On the Birmingham and East Warwickshire plateaux, where woodland and wasteland was of much greater extent, the majority of farmed land was enclosed in small hedged fields by the end of the period. Under the typical open-field system, the cultivated land was divided into two or three more or less equal fields. The land of each tenant farmer was held in long narrow strips regularly distributed across the two or three fields so that good and bad land were shared equally. In this way, too, the communal operations of ploughing and harvesting moved regularly from one man's strip to the next so that for each tenant some of his land was sown and harvested early, some in the peak of the season, and some late. The fields were cropped so that one or two were used for grain and the remaining one was rested, or fallowed, to restore its fertility. There was also an area of meadowland to provide early grazing and hay. Arable and meadow were thrown open for pasturing the animals of the villagers after harvest, while the fallow field was also used for pasture, the animals' manure helping to restore the fertility of the soil.

The villagers abided by a set of rules or 'customs' which regulated the crops which were to be sown, the fencing and grazing of stock, and the division of the meadow grass, and these rules were established and administered by the manorial court under the jurisdiction of the lord of the manor. Individual strips measured about 220 yards long by 26 yards wide and in area were usually between a quarter and a third of an acre. In south Warwickshire townships they were often divided from each other by a strip of grass some three or four feet wide, or sometimes by a deep furrow. The strips were grouped in rectangular furlongs and were arranged so that the furrows drained down the slope, important on the heavy clay soils of this region. Drainage could be further improved by ploughing the strip to form a hump-backed ridge, and over the years ridges could be built up to heights of six to eight feet in the centre. This was again a good form of insurance for the farmer since it ensured that in the wettest years there was some drier

37 *Sowing*

soil on the ridge top and in dry years the crops would grow well on the damper soils of the ridge flanks.

38   *Threshing*

The two-field system is thought to be the oldest form of common-field cultivation, and in south Warwickshire it was used until the 14th or 15th centuries. At Hampton Lucy, for example, the Bishop of Worcester in 1299 held an estate of nearly 300 acres in two fields called 'Overfelde' and 'Netherfelde', while two fields are recorded also in Harbury, Ladbroke, Brailes, Tysoe, Ettington, Tredington and Stratford. In the east of the county many townships reorganised their fields in the 13th and 14th centuries to give three fields so as to have a better rotation of crops and more land in cultivation. At Long Lawford, for example, two fields are recorded in the 13th century, but three by the 14th century. The manors of Coventry Cathedral Priory at Southam, Whitmore and Sowe were similarly organised around three fields in the 13th century. In south Warwickshire improved rotations and the pressure of population growth saw the division of the original two fields into four, while in the middle Avon valley the sub-division was even more complex with many townships having from five to eight fields by the 16th and 17th centuries. At Aston Cantlow there were two fields in 1273, for example; by 1348 this had become a three-field system, and subsequently a four- and then five-field system evolved. Similarly, for the small township of Kinwarton, a mid-18th-century plan reveals six fields. The main crops were wheat, sown in the winter for bread, spring-sown barley for making beer and, by the 13th century, an area for peas and beans. Cottage gardens provided other vegetables, such as leeks and cabbages, and chickens were kept for eggs and meat. Pigs were valuable for their meat products, while the better-off peasants would have had a milk cow to supplement their diet further.

39   *A six-ox plough team. Oxen were used for ploughing well into the 19th century in some areas. The medieval plough would have been made of wood and lacked a curved mould-board*

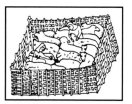

40 *A sheepfold*

Wood-Pasture Field Systems

In north and west Warwickshire the field and farming systems were rather different. There were areas of open-field cultivation especially in the lower Tame-Blythe valley where places such as Coleshill and Bickenhill had perhaps 25 per cent of their land in a regular three-field system. However, on the plateau areas around the oldest settlements, such as Tanworth-in-Arden, though there were open fields they normally constituted only 10 per cent or less of the township. These open-field cores were surrounded by an irregular patchwork of small embanked and hedged fields, cleared from the waste by migrant farmers and intermingled with the waste itself, which varied in character from grazed pasture, through heathland and scrub, to mature woodland. Pastoral farming was more important in this region; at Temple Balsall, for example, in 1308, an estate included 24 oxen, one bull, 22 cows, 24 young steers, 33 calves, five rams, 287 ewes, 212 lambs, two boars, five sows, 39 other pigs, 19 piglets, cart-horses, asses, mules, foals, doves, swans and peacocks! The estate, owned by the Knights Templar, was probably exceptional, but it illustrates well the difference in the emphasis of farming.

The 'champion' country of the Feldon had been long-settled and was already under intensive cultivation by Domesday times. In the succeeding three centuries population continued to grow, and by 1348, on the eve of the Black Death, Warwickshire's population had probably increased threefold.

41 *Sheep-shearing at Kingsbury. Sheep were an essential part of Warwickshire agriculture. Folded on the corn lands they manured the soil while their fleeces provided great wealth for monastic houses and Coventry merchants*

over that of 1086. At first, many champion parishes would have had small areas still to be brought into cultivation but, thereafter, the growing number of villagers could only be accommodated by dividing holdings, and the villein class could not do this. However, freeholders could do so, and there is evidence that strips were being divided into halves or thirds, as at Avon Dassett in the 13th and 14th centuries. The only other means of coping with the increasing number of people in south Warwickshire villages, since there was no major change in agricultural productivity, was through migration, and between the 12th and mid-14th centuries more and more people moved northwards into the Arden area of north and west Warwickshire, and from the villages to the towns. In the Arden region the majority of townships utilised perhaps 40 per cent or less of their land for agriculture in the 11th century, and so there was plenty of room for new farmers. Landowners were happy to accommodate these migrants and to grant them charters without enquiring too closely about their origins since they benefited from new money rents. By the mid-13th century, migrants were pouring into this area, and population growth in parishes like Tanworth-in-Arden or Stoneleigh showed a fourfold increase on that of 1086, and this trend was to continue into the 14th century. Migrants' surnames provide a valuable clue to distances travelled. The majority such as 'de Barford', 'de Radbourne', 'de Gaydon', and 'de Harbury' came from south Warwickshire and the Avon valley, but there were others from still further afield. There was a 'de Malverne' in Solihull, a 'de Cleobury' in Tanworth, and a 'de Bannebury' in Baddesley Clinton in the 13th century.

These migrant farmers became freeholders on their new farms and so, by the mid-13th century, there were distinctive regional differences in the social classes of Warwickshire's population. There were three main social classes among the common people: the free tenants enjoyed the highest legal status since they could leave the village if they wished and could sell or alienate their land as they wished. Villeins were not necessarily economically inferior to the freeman, but they held their land through doing labour services for their lord and could not alienate their land or leave the village without his permission. Finally, the cottagers had only their cottage, garden and perhaps an acre or two to support themselves, certainly not enough to live on, and so they had to supplement their income by working as labourers for other villagers, or by some craft. In the Feldon area perhaps 30 per cent of the population were free, 45 per cent of villein status and 25 per cent cottagers in the mid-13th century, whereas in Arden some 50 per cent were freemen, 25 per cent villeins, and 25 per cent cottagers. There were major differences, too, even within the classes. Labour services for the villeins, for example, varied enormously. In Arden, relatively few lords demanded more than light services, such as one or two days mowing and haymaking, or seasonal services such as ploughing, hoeing, or reaping to the extent of perhaps twenty to thirty days work by a tenant or his labourer. In the Feldon and Avon valley, however, not only did more lords demand seasonal services, but there were many who had the right to week-work from their villein tenants.

42   *Reaping*

43 *Medieval canon of St Mary's, Warwick*

44 *St Alphege's church, Solihull*

Such villeins had to work themselves, or provide the labour, for a fixed number of days throughout the year, and this was clearly a very heavy burden. Even so, the people of south Warwickshire were much better off than tenants in other parts of the county where labour services were still more onerous.

The Medieval Church

The Christian church played a major part in the social, economic and political history of Warwickshire from the seventh century through to the major upheaval of the Dissolution of the Monasteries in the reign of Henry VIII. The rites, festivals and feasts of the Church provided a focus for village social life; the Church as landowner demanded its rents and tithes, and many bishops, abbots and priests held positions of great secular political power.

Most of the 254 medieval churches in Warwickshire had been built by the early 13th century. The majority were parish churches deriving from earlier estate chapels, but some were constructed as dependent chapels of some earlier parish church to serve outlying communities in large parishes. In the large minster parish of Wootton Wawen there were dependent chapels at Henley-in-Arden and Ullenhall. Parish churches had to accommodate not only the needs of outlying communities but also the growing population of most settlements before the mid-13th century. Rebuilding and extension was thus going on all the time. Naves were lengthened, aisles added, and transepts constructed to enable more people to be accommodated for services. Where the local economy was prospering this could be done on a rather grander scale than elsewhere, but most churches shared in this rebuilding, especially between 1250 and 1350. The narrow, pointed arches of the Early English style are not a common feature of Warwickshire churches (the chancels of Pillerton Hersey and Northfield in Birmingham are the main examples) since most rebuilding and extending work took place when the curved tracery, larger windows and simpler piers of the Decorated style were in fashion. Changes in the style and size of churches in this period are most apparent in the older village centres and new market towns in the Arden region which were expanding most rapidly, such as Snitterfield, Tanworth-in-Arden, and the very large St Alphege's, Solihull, but other areas shared in the changes, including many in the Feldon where the expanding wool trade provided the financial stimulus.

The Black Death and the famines of the mid-14th century brought to an end the need to expand the size of churches. However, many sectors of the medieval economy recovered quite quickly, and some manorial lords, especially the new breed of capitalist farmers and merchants, wished to continue beautifying their parish churches. In the towns this often resulted in an almost complete rebuilding of the church in the fashionable new Perpendicular style. Holy Trinity and St Michael's in Coventry, St Mary's Warwick, Knowle, and the fine chancel of Stratford-on-Avon are examples.

In the countryside, village churches no longer required enlarging and so gifts were used to add towers to the west end of the church, or, in a few instances, to build a clerestory on the nave. The latter was a particular feature of the wool churches of the Cotswold fringe such as Brailes, Tysoe, Cherington, and Wormleighton, while towers were added to more than half Warwick-shire's churches in the 14th and 15th centuries. About two dozen of these also received spires, the majority in the north-east of the county, though perhaps the best known are the three spires which still grace the skyline of Coventry, and that at Stratford-on-Avon.

Another change in the late-medieval period was the fashion of erecting memorial chantry chapels within churches, an endowment providing income for a priest to say regular masses for the repose of the soul. Without doubt, the finest of these chapels is the Beauchamp Chapel in St Mary's, Warwick, begun in 1443 under the will of Richard Beauchamp, Earl of Warwick. It was completed in 1464 at a cost of nearly £2,500 and now contains the tombs of successive earls. Richard was buried in the centre of the chapel beneath a richly-carved tomb-chest of Purbeck marble with a gilded bronze effigy above. This is the crowning achievement of English 15th-century metalworking. There were chantries at Aston Cantlow, Atherstone-on-Stour, Brailes, Hampton-in-Arden, and Solihull among others.

Although much care was lavished upon church buildings and local crafts-men were able to use their skills to enliven the building with ornamentations, such as the animals and dragons dancing round the top of the piers of Burton Dassett, or the carvings under the choir stall seats at Stratford, the

45 *Brailes church, mainly 15th-century*

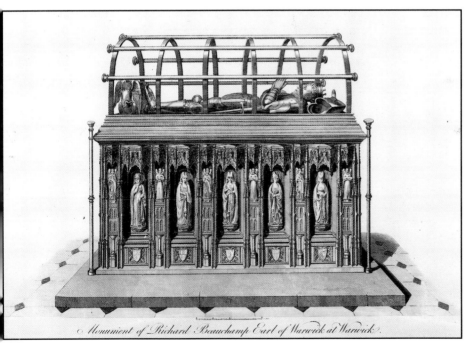

Monument of Richard Beauchamp Earl of Warwick at Warwick.

46 *The monument of Richard Beauchamp, Earl of Warwick. Richard died in 1439; his chantry chapel in St Mary's, Warwick is one of the richest in England. the tomb is of Purbeck marble and the effigy and figures in copper-gilt are the crowning achievement of English 15th-century metalcraft*

47 *Hatton church, c.1800. Except for the tower, the parish church of Holy Trinity, Hatton was rebuilt in 1880. The Aylesford drawings in Birmingham Reference Library show most Warwickshire churches before such Victorian restoration and reconstruction*

people were often poorly served by their priests. The rector's income came from tithes of the agricultural produce, from the fees for baptisms, marriage and burial, from offerings, and from the glebe land which belonged to the church. The larger the parish, therefore, the larger his income tended to be. However, the rector's income was often gifted to a monastery who then instituted a vicar to look after the spiritual needs of the people, paying him only a small proportion of the income. Low incomes meant that poorly-qualified men were drawn into many vicarages, while the rectories of the small parishes were worth only a little more. Even the parishes where the rectorial income was more substantial were not always well-served since these were often held in plurality. William de Marchia, though only a sub-deacon, was rector of Mancetter in 1291 in combination with seven other churches spread the length and breadth of the country, and Robert de Toorpe was rector of both Rugby and three other churches in the same year. By the 16th century, 89 of Warwickshire's rectories were held by monastic institutions, the largest number (17) being held by Kenilworth Priory. Coventry Priory held five churches; Arbury and Warwick collegiate church four each; and Nuneaton three. Other churches were held by institutions outside the county, including four by Lichfield Cathedral Chapter.

The Monasteries

The oldest monastic house in Warwickshire was the great Benedictine priory of Coventry, founded by the Saxon Earl Leofric and his wife, Godgifu (Godiva) in 1043. It was richly endowed with a score of manors in Warwickshire and

V *Holy Trinity, Stratford-upon-Avon. This early minster church served the Bishop of Worcester's great estate at Stratford. It was made collegiate in 1331 by Bishop John de Stratford. The fine Perpendicular chancel was built in the 1490s and contains the monument to William Shakespeare.*

VI *The Gild Chapel and Grammar School, Stratford-upon-Avon. The Gild of the Holy Cross was Stratford's most important social institution. The chapel is late 15th-century and contains a 'Doom' wall painting. The Grammar School was built in 1417 as the Guildhall. Beyond in Chapel Street, the 'Tudor' façade of Nash's House dates from 1912. The five gables of the* Shakespeare Hotel *represent the width of an original burgage of three-and-a-half perches.*

others elsewhere in the Midlands, including Grandborough, Honington, Bishop's Itchington, and Priors Hardwick. The diocesan see was transferred to Coventry in 1102 and the bishops of the diocese were considered the titular abbots of the monastery. At the Dissolution it had an annual rental of just over £800 per year. There was a second Benedictine abbey at Alcester, founded in 1140 but it was very small and, in 1465, was absorbed into the great Worcestershire house at Evesham, while a third small priory at Alvecote, in the extreme north, was a cell of Malvern Abbey. Four small priories were cells of foreign Benedictine houses and were confiscated to the crown in the 14th and 15th centuries. There were small priories of nuns at Henwood, Wroxall and Polesworth, the latter, though refounded soon after the Conquest, after a temporary sojourn in Oldbury, being perhaps the only priory to survive the Danish destructions of 1016. It had been founded by King Egbert in the 9th century and was dedicated to his saint-daughter, Editha, who was one

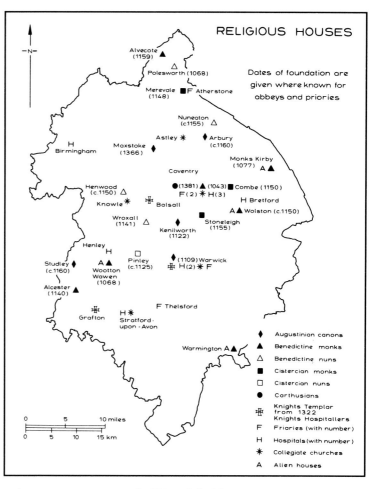

48 *Religious houses in Warwickshire*

of the first abbesses. However, the most important nunnery in Warwickshire was that at Nuneaton, founded in the mid-12th century by Robert, Earl of Leicester, as a cell of the great abbey at Fontevrault. It had a value of over £250 in 1535.

There were three abbeys of the white-robed Cistercians in Warwickshire: Coombe, Merevale, and Stoneleigh, and a small priory of nuns at Pinley, all founded in the mid-12th century and all actively engaged in clearing forest and waste lands on their north Warwickshire estates. Stoneleigh seems to have suffered a number of adverse circumstances. In 1241 it was badly damaged by fire so the king gave the monks 40 oaks from his woods at Kenilworth to help with the repairs. In 1258, both abbey and estates were attacked by an armed gang who set fire to houses, burnt the abbey gatehouse, broke into the park and killed the deer; while in 1380 the abbey seal was stolen by one Roger de Kirketon, who used it to sell some of the abbey's property. The monks were not altogether blameless, however, and there were a number of enquiries into the lax running of the house in the 13th and 14th centuries.

49 *Medieval lady from a destroyed brass*

The only Carthusian priory was St Anne's, Coventry, founded by William, Lord Zouch in 1381. The Carthusians lived by themselves in separate cells within the monastery, rather than communally. Its fortunes were considerably boosted by the interest of Richard II, who laid the foundation stone of the church in 1385, so that despite its late foundation it was valued at over £200 in 1536, and King Henry's Commissioners reported that the 12 brethren and prior were 'in virtue, contemplation and religion excellent'. Besides the brothers there were three lay-brothers, six servants, and 12 poor children being educated there. There were five Augustinian houses, all but Maxstoke Priory being founded in the 12th century. Undoubtedly the most important was the great priory at Kenilworth, founded in 1122 by Geoffrey de Clinton, Chamberlain and Treasurer to Henry I, and raised to the rank of abbey in the 15th century.

The Orders of Friars were a product of 13th-century dissatisfaction with the increasing wealth of the established monastic orders. The friars wished to follow a simple evangelistic life and their adherence to strict vows of poverty effectively restricted them to the larger towns. Franciscans were established in Coventry by 1234 and Carmelites by 1342; the Dominicans had a friary in Warwick by 1263 and the Austin Friars a house in Atherstone, established in 1375. The only rural friary was the Trinitarian house at Thelsford, near Stratford-on-Avon. The poverty of the friars appealed particularly to the aristocracy and rich merchants and each of the Warwickshire friaries was founded by persons of considerable wealth, such as Sir John Poultney, a merchant and one-time Lord Mayor of London, who founded the Carmelite friary at Coventry.

Feudal Castles

Warfare was endemic in medieval society. The whole system of landholding which is generally termed 'feudal' was an arrangement by which an overlord granted land to tenants for a variety of personal services as a form of rent. Some were agricultural, but one such service was almost always military. Tenants could appear in person when requested, suitably armed and equipped according to their status or, from the late 12th century onwards, a money rent could be substituted. In turn, the overlords and barons held their estates from the king for so many 'knights fees' by which they had to provide the requisite number of armed knights and retainers for the king's army when called to do so. Wars with France and Scotland, the conquest of Wales, the Crusades, and a number of civil wars caused by the rebellions of powerful barons and the breakdown of central authority, such as occurred during the reigns of Stephen and John, meant that military power was of continuing significance.

Warwickshire, in the very heart of England, could take little direct part in foreign wars, but was of some strategic importance in any internal disturbance. However, there are only two castles of the first rank in the county: Warwick, the centre of one of the great feudal estates of medieval

50 *Warwick Castle from the south east in 1729. The towers at the east end were built by Thomas Beauchamp and his son in the mid-14th century. The medieval bridge was partially removed in the 1790s*

England, and Kenilworth, a bare five miles distant, which provided a royal base to balance and watch over the baronial power. There are, however, a very large number of lesser castles and fortified manors in Warwickshire and they show how necessary it was for lesser lords to be able to defend themselves against neighbours. When legal authority was far away in London and travel was slow and sometimes dangerous, raiding, looting, and rustling were not uncommon, while arguments and quarrels would be often settled by force of arms.

The first castle built in Warwickshire was the great motte and bailey at Warwick itself, constructed immediately after the Conquest as part of King William's policy of planting castles in all the Anglo-Saxon towns to overawe and control these obvious centres of dissent. Other lords followed as they took over rural properties. Where such places continued as residences, the cramped early castles were rebuilt on a grander scale and timber palisades were replaced by stone, as at Hartshill and Baginton. Other small and temporary motte and bailey castles were thrown up during the civil war between Stephen and Matilda in the 12th century and during the troubled years of John's reign.

The great castle at Kenilworth was established by Geoffrey de Clinton, Chamberlain to Henry I, in about 1125. He and his son built an oval, bailey-like enclosure which was defended by damming streams to create a great lake to the south and west, and which supplied a broad moat on the remaining sides. Within the bailey a great stone keep was built with walls 20ft. thick at the base. Kenilworth was commandeered by Henry II in 1173-4 and, in 1182, the de Clintons exchanged the castle for lands in Buckinghamshire. King John spent the large sum of £2,000 on the castle to provide the curtain wall and towers, and the effectiveness of the new defences was proved during the rebellion of Simon de Montfort, to whom Henry III had granted the castle in 1255. After the battle of Evesham, for more than a

51 The ruins of Kenilworth Castle. Kenilworth was defended by a great lake which was drained in the Civil Wars. The Earl of Leicester had spent a fortune on the castle and gardens to entertain Elizabeth I

year, Kenilworth defied repeated attacks by siege towers, battering rams and fortified barges sent across the mere, and the garrison only surrendered when they were reduced to eating their horses. In the late 14th century Kenilworth was held by the wealthy and ostentatious John of Gaunt, Duke of Lancaster, who began converting it from a feudal stronghold into a palace by adding the Great Hall. The process was taken a stage further by Queen Elizabeth's favourite, Robert Dudley, Earl of Leicester in the 1570s.

A similar process of improving the fortifications and then of conversion to a more comfortable mansion took place at Warwick. The two great towers, Caesar's and Guy's, the gatehouse and the high curtain wall at the east end of the castle date from the second half of the 14th century and were built by Thomas Beauchamp and his son, also Thomas, who were probably also responsible for improving the main range of domestic buildings on the south side including the Great Hall. The accounts for Guy's Tower survive. It was completed in 1394 at a cost of £395 5s. 2d. Warwick Castle was the site of the demise of Piers Gaveston, the favourite of Edward II. He had been seized by Guy Beauchamp in 1312. He was brought to Warwick and after some debate was taken to Blacklowe Hill for execution.

Moated Houses

Great castles were in a minority in the later medieval period, while even the small motte and baileys had been largely abandoned by about 1215. Far more ubiquitous as the home of a lesser feudal lord or of his free tenants was the moated homestead. Moated houses range from the fortified homes of the lesser aristocracy, such as Maxstoke Castle, built by Sir William Clinton in 1346, with corner towers, embattled curtain walls, gatehouse, and broad surrounding moat, down to the ordinary farmhouse and garden ground of a free tenant farmer colonising the waste in Arden. There are hundreds of these moated sites in Warwickshire, the majority of them in the latter class. They are characteristically located in the north-west of the county where lords were actively encouraging new tenants to clear farms from the heath and woodland in the period between 1150 and 1350. The majority of the parishes in this region have one or two moated farms while Tanworth-in-Arden has no less than twelve. The moat served a number of functions;

52 *Maxstoke Castle*

53 *Castles and moats in Warwickshire*

it was certainly defensive, helping to keep marauding bands of soldiers out of gardens and barns in times of strife, besides brigands and poachers at other times. It also kept deer and rabbits out of the orchards and vegetable garden. The moat provided additional resources since it would be used as a fish-pond, a swannery, or for ducks. It was certainly a status symbol in the later medieval period, indicating the farmer's independence; this was his 'manor house' at the centre of his small farm laboriously cleared from the waste by himself or his ancestors. Finally, it might well have helped provide a drier farmyard in wet winters since the island on which the farm stood was raised above its surroundings with the material dug from making the moat.

From about 1450, moats began to be less fashionable and at many sites were abandoned for new timber-framed farmhouses, or stone mansions a short distance away. At first the moat might have continued in use as a fish-pond, but eventually many were drained. Perhaps one of

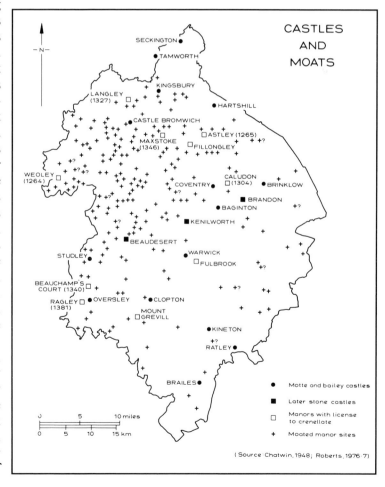

CASTLES AND MOATS

- SECKINGTON
- TAMWORTH
- KINGSBURY
- LANGLEY (1327)
- HARTSHILL
- CASTLE BROMWICH
- ASTLEY (1265)
- MAXSTOKE (1346)
- FILLONGLEY
- WEOLEY (1264)
- CALUDON (1304)
- COVENTRY
- BRINKLOW
- BRANDON
- BAGINTON
- KENILWORTH
- BEAUDESERT
- STUDLEY
- WARWICK
- FULBROOK
- BEAUCHAMP'S COURT (1340)
- RAGLEY (1381)
- OVERSLEY
- CLOPTON
- MOUNT GREVILL
- KINETON
- RATLEY
- BRAILES

5   10 miles

0   5   10   15 km

- ● Motte and bailey castles
- ■ Later stone castles
- ☐ Manors with license to crenellate
- + Moated manor sites

(Source: Chatwin, 1948; Roberts, 1976-7)

54 *Baddesley Clinton moated manor house*

the last to be created was the perfect late-medieval manor house at Baddesley Clinton, built in the mid-15th century by the Ferrers family and relatively little altered subsequently. Coughton Court was similar when built by the Throckmortons in the early 15th century, but the house was substantially altered and extended in the 16th century, and the moat subsequently filled in. There is a fine abandoned site at Moreton Bagot with only a timbered barn left on the island; the farm was rebuilt in the late 16th century a little distance away.

Deer Parks

Most of the larger castles in Warwickshire and many of the larger manors, particularly in the northern half of the county, had a deer park as part of their demesne lands. Sometimes, as at Beaudesert, it surrounded the castle, but more frequently it was located towards the edge of the manor where the lords were able to make parks from the waste without interfering with agricultural land. Parks varied greatly in size from as little as forty or fifty acres, to several thousand acres in the case of the Earl of Warwick's great park at Wedgenock. They were preserved as open grazing and woodland primarily for the protection and maintenance of a herd of deer, which could then be hunted for the pleasure of its lord. To enclose the deer and keep poachers out, parks were surrounded by bank and ditch and on top of the bank a stout oak pale fence or, more rarely, a wall was made. Deer provided not only sport for the lord, but were also an important source of meat. The sport could always be made more exciting by poaching deer from neighbouring parks so that poachers were by no means always oppressed peasants seeking food for starving families. A high proportion of those arrested for poaching were well-to-do, and even the clergy were not averse to joining in such forays.

Parks contained more than deer, however. The majority were also used for grazing cattle and, in the later medieval period, lords could obtain considerable money rents by letting their park pastures to capitalist graziers. The woods were a source of profit, too, and were normally carefully managed; the mature timber in Fernhill Wood, in Wedgenock Park, for instance, was sold for £2,000 in 1590, and the coppice was then enclosed to protect it from browsing deer. Woods were often the source of timber for major building projects such as churches or manor houses; at Beaudesert timber felled in the park was used to repair the hall of the castle. Many parks also contained fish-ponds since the enclosure provided the best protection against poachers. The fish-ponds were often linked to a moated house either for the park keeper, in the case of the larger parks, or the actual manor house. The Earl of Chester's manor at Coventry was early removed from the town-centre castle to a moated manor on the edge of Cheylesmore Park, while at Warwick the earl maintained a large moated house at Goodrest, within Wedgenock Park, as a rural retreat. There was a similar retreat in Kenilworth Park, the Plaisaunce, built by Henry V and provided with a timber-framed banqueting

55 *Warwick seal*

ouse. Some idea of what these deer parks looked like can still be gained today from the wilder parts of the great park at Sutton Coldfield, which was one of the deer parks of the Earl of Warwick until purchased by Bishop Vesey for the town in the 16th century.

One last activity that must find mention is again connected with Kenilworth, since the park was one of the five licensed tournament grounds in England where knights could meet together to display their prowess. In the 12th and 13th centuries jousting was a serious and often bloody affair in which teams of knights charged in an open mêlée. There were few rules and great personal danger. Such 'sport' was legalised by Richard I in 1194 and provided the opportunity for landless knights to gain fame and fortune. In the later medieval period jousting became formalised into the tournaments watched by courtiers and ladies. Such a tournament was held in 1279 by Edmund, Earl of Lancaster, 100 knights taking part, and the great dam which retained the mere was used as the tilt yard.

Towns, Markets and Fairs

In 1086 the only towns in Warwickshire were Warwick, Tamworth and, probably, Coventry. By 1450 some forty markets had been established and approximately half had developed sufficiently to attain the status of a borough. These towns were recognisably different from other settlements in both their appearance and in the sort of people who lived there. Most were larger than neighbouring villages; they had a more complex network of streets and lanes; there was an open space where the market was held each week; churches were often large, and there could be other religious institutions such as friaries and hospitals, while most characteristic of all was the pattern of long, narrow tenements which lined the streets. The houses and workshops formed a continuous line of buildings and the plots were sometimes so regular in size as to have been obviously planned.

The inhabitants of the towns looked to crafts and industry and trade for their living. Though they might hold a few acres of land in the town fields, and grow vegetables, and keep a pig on the back land of their tenement, this was for their own sustenance. The great majority of the town-dwellers were free. They held their tenement for a fixed annual money rent, did not have to work in the fields for the lord, and could dispose of their property as they wished. In the largest boroughs the townspeople became a self-governing community by the later medieval period, notably in Coventry, and by Tudor times in Stratford, Tamworth and Warwick.

Clearly this rapid growth of markets and boroughs, not just in Warwickshire, but all over England, was associated with the growing population and economic prosperity of the 13th century. For lords, towns could be a source of great profit since not only was there money rents from the tenements, but usually market tolls and court fines could be collected as well. Lords, therefore, vied with each other to establish successful markets and it is not surprising to find that the Crown was early involved in bringing some order

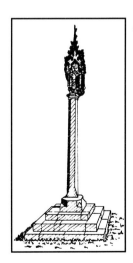

56 *Market cross at Henley-in-Arden*

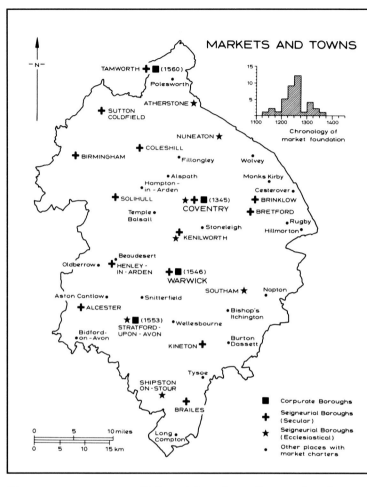

MARKETS AND TOWNS

Chronology of market foundation

Corporate Boroughs

Seigneurial Boroughs (Secular)

Seigneurial Boroughs (Ecclesiastical)

Other places with market charters

57 *The markets and towns of medieval Warwickshire*

to this scene. Most lords sought charter from the Crown to safe guard their new-founded town. New markets were not normall allowed nearer than six and two thirds miles from an established one and adjacent markets were usuall on a different day of the week. Thi distance was reckoned an averag day's journey for anyone wantin to buy or sell in the market an return home. Thus, in sout Warwickshire, there were market at Brailes on Monday, Kineton o Tuesday, Tysoe on Wednesda Stratford on Thursday, Burto Dassett on Friday, and Shipston on-Stour on Saturday. Such a pat tern enabled itinerant traders t move from market to market on regular weekly basis. This densit of market provision could only b sustained with a high populatio After the mid-14th-century plagu many of the smaller and less we situated markets went out of us In places such as Brailes, Tyso Polesworth and Bishop's Itchingto it is only the open space of th former market place whic distinguishes them from other large villages in the region.

The earliest of the newly-chartered markets were established in the mid-12t century, all in the west of Warwickshire, at Stratford-on-Avon, Beaudeser and Birmingham. At Stratford, the Bishop of Worcester, John de Coutance obtained a market charter in 1196, from Richard I, and almost immediatel advanced it to the status of a borough. The town was planned on a gran scale with a grid of streets laid out between the earlier village and the ol Roman street which gave name to the place. The inhabitants were grante their tenements at an annual rent of 12d., the plots being some sixty feet wid and 200ft. long, or about a quarter of an acre in area. This was more tha sufficient to build two or three houses along the street front, and so most o these plots were quickly sub-divided into halves or thirds as more and mor people came to settle in the bishop's new town.

The surnames of these early inhabitants give a clue to where they wer coming from. Most came from within fifteen miles of the new town an especially from south Warwickshire and the Vale of Evesham, where village were already over-populated: men such as Bardolfus de Chesterton and Walter de Clifford. Indeed, many, such as Reginald de Tiddington and William de Wilncote, came from the bishop's own rural estates around Stratford. Others came from older-established boroughs, such as John de Evesham, John de Campden, and Henry de Leicester. These men might have been established traders. The names give a clue, too, to some of the occupations of the townspeople: there were ropemakers, coopers, mercers, tailors, carpenters, butchers, and, most numerous, tanners. With the advantage of the river trade, an important ford with roads focusing on it and a location mid-way between the developing pastoral economy of Arden and the grain-growing communities of Feldon, the new town flourished. On market days the traders filled streets and market place. There were stalls for dairy products, and butchers in the broad market of Bridge Street; corn was sold in what is now Chapel Street, and cattle were bought and sold in a separate market place on the edge of the town—the Rother Market.

The foundation of Birmingham offers a complete contrast. Whereas Stratford was founded by an important lord at the centre of a prosperous estate in one of the richest parts of the shire, Birmingham was established on a small, relatively infertile estate owned by a family of no great distinction. The one advantage they shared was their early foundation. Peter de Birmingham obtained his market charter in 1154 and the place had become a borough by the early 13th century. Again, men were moving into the new town from the immediately surrounding regions, but in Birmingham there

58 *Henley-in-Arden. The medieval new town at Henley was developed by the de Montfort family along the Birmingham-Stratford road. Many 17th-century timber-framed houses line the broad market street. Coaching brought a brief prosperity to the town between 1790 and 1840*

59 *The five gables of the* Shakespeare Hotel, *Stratford*

was no grand planned town, new tenements were simply fenced off along existing lanes wherever there was room. These lanes focused onto the all-important market place, the great triangular Bull Ring with the parish church set in its midst, and stalls and butchers' shambles stretching up the hill on the road to Walsall. It seems probable that this was the village green before Birmingham became a town.

The main period of market founding was between 1220 and 1270. Towns founded by secular lords include Brailes and Sutton Coldfield by the Earls of Warwick, Henley-in-Arden, founded by Peter de Montfort in 1220, and Kenilworth founded by the builder of Kenilworth Castle, Geoffrey de Clinton. A second borough was founded at Kenilworth by the Augustinian Priory, the two parts of the town, each with their own market place, being separated by the priory church and its great fish-pond. Other ecclesiastical boroughs include Nuneaton, where the nuns of the Benedictine priory laid out a planned borough between the village and the abbey in the early 13th century; Shipston-on-Stour, founded by Worcester Priory, and Atherstone, another planned town laid out along Watling Street by the Norman abbey of Bec in the mid-13th century. Coventry Priory was still trying to promote the development of Southam in the late 14th century by laying out a new market place and tenements north of the older town, but such optimism in the period after the Black Death is unusual, and many places declined. Bretford, a borough founded by the de Verdons, lords of Brandon Castle in 1227, where the Fosse Way crossed the Avon, declined absolutely, and only a farm and cottage mark the site today. Other south Warwickshire towns fared almost as badly, while even

60 *Coleshill High Street, c.1900. A typical 'street' borough, Coleshill had been laid out on either side of the highway between Coventry and Lichfield in the early 13th century. The large parish church is more ancient, however, and there is the site of a Roman temple nearby*

in the more prosperous Avon valley and the fast-developing Arden region towns such as Henley-in-Arden and Stratford suffered much decline so that tenements away from the town centre were abandoned to pasture closes.

It was in this period, too, that the inhabitants of boroughs with ecclesiastical overlords, who tended to maintain a more rigid control, came to demand greater freedom. There were riots in Shipston in the first years of the 15th century over a dispute between the Prior of Worcester and his tenants and the town's fair was discontinued as a result.

61 *Medieval merchant's house, Warwick*

The borough of Warwick in the medieval period was not greatly different from the other towns of the shire despite its status as the county town. It is one of the few medieval county towns that was not incorporated, the Charter of Incorporation being obtained only in 1546. Though it remained under the control of the Earls of Warwick, restrictions were few and successive earls did all in their power to encourage the economic well-being of the town, but it did not flourish. Thomas Beauchamp provided a booth hall in the market place and made the town free of toll in 1359, while Richard, his grandson, planned to make the Avon navigable up to Warwick. The town was walled because of its strategic position beside Warwick Castle, and there were gates to the east and west, both of which were surmounted by chapels. The medieval bridge below the castle ramparts was also gated. There were extensive suburbs outside the walls which were administered separately, and some of the richest Warwick merchants lived there rather than in the town centre. The town had a guild from 1383, who were responsible for the upkeep of bridge and highways; several hospitals (including the leper hospital of St Michael's, whose buildings form a unique survival in Saltisford suburb), and churches, besides the shire court and gaol. To John Leland in about 1540, 'the beauty and glory of the towne is in 2 strets; whereof the one is callyd the Highe Strete having a right goodly crosse in the middle of it. The other crossith the middle of it, and goith from northe to southe'. The parish church of St Mary was 'faire and large' and the town 'hathe bene right strongly dyked and waulyd'. Over the west gate was 'a goodly chappell of St James' with 'a pretty colledge having 4 preistes that sing', but dominating the town then, as now, was 'the magnificent and stronge castle of Warwick sett upon an highe rokke of stone'.

62 *West gate, Warwick*

Medieval Coventry

The foundation of a new Benedictine abbey in 1043, on the site of a nunnery which had been sacked in the Danish raids of 1016, marks the beginning of Coventry's rise to prosperity. The abbey was founded by Leofric, Earl of Mercia, and his wife Godiva, and they endowed it with extensive estates so that it became one of the richest foundations in the Midlands. Probably very soon afterwards a market had been established at the abbey gates and a small town began to develop. By the beginning of the 12th century the growing settlement at the gates of the abbey was being served by two churches: Holy

63 *Gosford Gate, Coventry*

Trinity, fronting on to the market place, provided so that the monks did not have to share the abbey church with the townspeople, and St Nicholas's in the suburb of Radford, a dependent chapelry. The prosperity of the abbey had encouraged the Bishop of Chester to transfer the diocesan see to Coventry, probably in 1095, and Bishop Robert de Limesey took the opportunity of the abbot's death to instal himself as abbot. The abbey thus became a cathedral priory. One reason for his move from Chester was to establish an episcopal estate separate from those of the Norman Earls of Chester. Coventry was part of the earl's estate, but was far distant from Chester. The earl was a minor at the time of Robert de Limesey's move to Coventry and the bishop seized the opportunity to secure his hold on the northern parts of the town by means of a series of forged charters. The town around and to the north of the market place thus became an ecclesiastical borough with all the disadvantages of close control that this implied.

The southern half of the town seems to have developed beside a ringwork castle, constructed by the Earl of Chester around, and to the south of the minster church of St Michael. The castle is documented for the period from

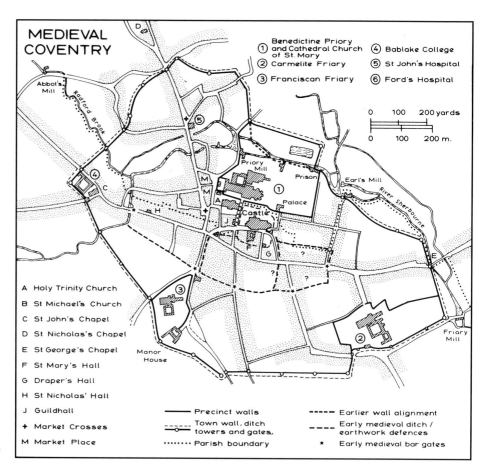

64 *Medieval Coventry*

1144 to the early 13th century, though it could have been built as early as about 1088 when the Earls of Chester gained their Coventry estates. A substantial defensive ditch, usually called the Red Ditch in contemporary documents, enclosed the properties along High Street and Earl Street by the 12th century and linked them to the castle and, as the suburbs east and west of the defences were rapidly built up along Smithford Street and Jordan Well, the ditches were extended to enclose them. Southwards was the earl's park of Cheylesmore and, by 1200, the castle was passing out of use in favour of a manor house in the park. Bailey Lane provided access for later development on the castle site.

Ranulph de Gerdons granted the earl's town its first charter in about 1150. It gave the townspeople their own court and the burgage tenure of their property. The woollen textile trade was already the foundation of the town's prosperity and growth. Fulling mills were established on the river Sherborne and the Radford Brook and altogether there were more than a dozen mills in the 12th-century town. The various branches of woollen cloth manufacture were concentrated along the main east-west street of the earl's part of the town where there were also carters and goldsmiths. Masons, carpenters, thatchers, bakers, and butchers were established throughout the town, while tanners and leather-workers lived in the outer suburbs. In the prior's part of the town there were weavers, dyers and metal workers, as well as one or two merchants.

By 1200 the prosperity of the town required new building and so first Much Park Street and then Little Park Street were developed on land taken from Cheylesmore Park. About 1230, Earl Ranulf III granted another portion of the park to the Franciscan friars for their church and house. The

65 *The city of Coventry in 1760. Coventry was still largely contained within its medieval walls in 1760 and the prospect was dominated by the three church spires of the Friary (5), Holy Trinity (9) and St Michael's (10)*

66 *Butcher Row, Coventry, c.1905. A narrow market shambles in the heart of the city. Many late medieval timber-framed buildings survived into the 20th century but were obliterated in the great air raid of November 1940*

67 *Bablake Hospital and St John's Guild Church, Coventry*

Whitefriars (Carmelites) did not come to Coventry until 1342, but their precinct with its large church and extensive grounds and orchards enclosed nearly ten acres south of Gosford Street. The priory lands were also being further developed. Properties were established on the market place and a new street was laid out across former orchard land. West Orchard allowed visitors to the priory to enter without passing through the earl's half of the town.

Meanwhile, the merchants were growing in number and importance and by 1300 were engaged in the international wool trade with Flanders. They lived mostly in the very centre of the town, in Earl Street. The city's prosperity rested particularly upon the dyers who produced the famous 'Coventry blue' cloth with its non-fading qualities. It is not surprising to find that the merchants were unwilling to submit to the control of the prior and the 13th century witnessed a long struggle between the prior and his monks and the merchants of the earl's part of the town for control of the markets, fairs and courts. In 1330, the earl's manor was devolved upon Queen Isabella. With her help, the men of Coventry obtained freedom from tolls on their goods throughout the country, their own guild merchant and many judicial rights. In 1345, Edward III granted the town its first Charter of Incorporation, so that henceforth it was governed by a mayor and bailiffs and the influence of the priory came to an end. By the second half of the 15th century the townspeople had freed themselves from both manorial and county jurisdictions and in 1451 this was confirmed when Henry VI granted a charter which made the city and its environs a county in itself.

Work began on Coventry's town wall in the 1350s at the instigation of mayor Richard de Stoke. Building began with New Gate at the bottom of Much Park Street. Most of the gates and towers were completed by 1400, but parts of the wall around the north of the town were still being built nearly a century later. They were financed by a special tax called murage, and most of the stone was dug on site, thereby helping to provide the external ditch. The 14th century was a great period of building activity elsewhere in the city. St Mary's Hall was begun for the guild merchant in 1340, while Bablake College and chapel was built in 1350 for the newly-founded St John's Guild on land given by Queen Isabella. Holy Trinity church had been destroyed by fire in 1257 and was rebuilt as a large cruciform building, while St Michael's was largely rebuilt and considerably enlarged in the 1350s. The new choir and graceful steeple were financed by the Botoner

68 *St Michael's, Coventry, 1730. The surveyor and scientist, Henry Beighton, drew this north prospect of St Michael's. This fine 300-ft. high tower and steeple was built between 1371 and c.1430. St Michael's became the cathedral in 1918 and was gutted in the 1940 bombing*

69 *St Mary's Hall and stocks*

family, who had built their fortune from the wool trade. However, the enlarged church was built over the long forgotten Red Ditch. As a result the new tower subsided into the infill materials and the spire was built with a kink to try to counteract the lean of the tower. In about 1400, St Mary's Hall was enlarged for the guild of the Holy Trinity and the great hall with its fine timber roof, heraldic bosses and tapestries was built. At the same time merchants were building themselves large timber-framed houses with stone-vaulted cellars below in which to store their merchandise. In the 14th century the city became even more dependent upon the cloth trade and perhaps half the merchants and craftsmen living there gained their living in this way.

By 1400, the craft guilds monopolised trade in the city, and each had their guild hall and chapel. The 10 most important guilds also took part of the cycle of mystery plays performed at Corpus Christi-tide. Each play was presented on a stage, mounted on a wagon at a traditional site, one in each of the 10 wards of the city. The mercers, drapers, weavers, fullers, pinners, needlers, shearmen, and tailors were among those who took part in these pageants. However, they were costly to mount and during the 16th century, as the cloth trade went into a deep recession, other guilds joined in to support this important part of city life, most notably the cappers.

The Textile and Coal Industries

Early industrial prosperity was based on the wool trade and upon textile manufacture, and branches of this industry continued to be of significance until the late 19th century. Wool merchants came to prominence in the mid-14th century following the formation of the Staple Company. The Staple operated a monopoly over the sale of English wool overseas in return for a large cash payment to the Exchequer and some of the most important wool merchants were Warwickshire men. The majority were based in Coventry, but there were also important merchants in Warwick, and in Birmingham, including Walter de Clodshale and John Atte Holte, the family who were later to establish themselves at Aston Hall. In Coventry the two merchants who stand out prominently are Jordan de Shepeye and Thomas de Toltham. These men became very rich on the proceeds of their trade and had property and land in London and the Continental ports as well as in Coventry. Most wool was exported through London, though some went east to Boston. The mercantile links between Coventry and London were very strong and Warwickshire merchants were elected Lord Mayor of London on a number of occasions. In Coventry the mayoralty was held by wool merchants 19 times between 1349 and 1377.

It was during this period that the English cloth industry was expanding and, in Warwickshire, it was again Coventry that came rapidly to the fore as both a marketing and production centre. During 1398, for example, nearly 1,500 full-sized cloths, 24 yards in length, were sold, and some 3,300 'dozens', or half-length cloths. The second largest market was Birmingham where a mere 88 dozens were sold, while there were less than half this quantity at other markets such as Warwick, Henley, Alcester, and Southam. Certainly some of this cloth would have been manufactured in the villages, particularly in the region around Coventry, but a very high proportion was made in Coventry itself where many of the finishing processes were also concentrated. In 1449, the Coventry Leet Book lists 59 master drapers, 57 weavers, 28 fullers, 37 dyers, and 64 tailors and shearmen.

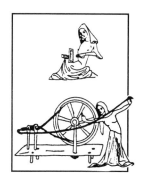

70 *Women spinning and carding*

The earliest documentary record of coal mining in Warwickshire is from 1275, but mining was certainly taking place rather earlier as the coalfield was worked in Roman times. Indeed, it is possible that Griff, near Nuneaton, gets its place-name from early coal-pits since the name derives from the Norse word for a pit or hole. There are many medieval references to mining in the Nuneaton area in the documents relating to the priory. In 1350, the prioress made complaint that seven named individuals had 'with armed force dug in the private land of the priory ... and had carried away thence sea coal to the value of £40'. Another frequent cause of complaint in the medieval period was the failure of miners to fill in worked-out pits. The pits were mostly shallow surface diggings and as the coal was removed the pit was filled in and a new one begun. They rarely exceeded a dozen feet in depth. Coal was a source of some profit to Nuneaton priory in the 14th century, but by the early 16th century most of the surface deposits had been worked out. All these medieval references are to the areas of Chilvers Coten, Stockingford, and Haunchwood, south of Nuneaton. However, it seems likely that coal was also worked near Coventry. Certainly it was sold there in substantial quantities, as in 1469 the mayor prohibited coal carts from entering the city on market days because of the congestion they caused.

6

Desertion, Dissolution and Civil War, 1485-1660

The grass-grown humps and depressions of a former village site, an isolated parish church, and the great ditch of an abandoned moated manor, all surrounded by the ridge and furrow of medieval open fields was, until very recently, one of the most characteristic landscapes of the south Warwickshire countryside. In parish after parish in the Feldon, these 'lost' villages and hamlets tell of manorial lords who enclosed their land for pasturing sheep or cattle, allowed cottages to fall down, people to drift away to other villages or the town, and the parish church to decay. That story is primarily set in the century between 1450 and 1550.

Deserted Settlements

Settlements had been deserted in an earlier age—following the Conquest, for example, when the lands of rebellious lords or of whole regions were 'wasted' by the Norman troops as punishment, but these settlements were normally re-populated, and farming had begun again within half a century. Similarly, the founding of Cistercian abbeys at Coombe and Stoneleigh in the mid-12th century had necessitated the removal of settlements. The Cistercian rule demanded that their abbeys enjoy a rural and isolated location and, whereas that was relatively easy to find in the Yorkshire Dales, there was little empty and uncultivated land in Warwickshire. The foundation of Coombe Abbey in 1150 led to the depopulation of the two villages of Upper and Lower Smite, and eventually even to the replacement of the parish name by that of Coombe, while at Stoneleigh, founded in 1154, the monks 'settled in the place where Crulefield Grange now is, having moved away those who lived there to the village now called Hurst'. Further depopulation was to follow in early Tudor times at Stoneleigh. Another desertion linked to the Cistercians was Cawston-on-Dunsmore which was developed as the principal grange of Pipewell Abbey, Northamptonshire from 1201.

    The Black Death and the poor harvests and famines which preceded it in the early 14th century were long looked upon as a prime cause of the desertion of settlements. However, very few villages were totally abandoned as a direct result of the plague. Rather, these events set in train a process of change which culminated a century later in the abandonment of whole villages. The number of people in many settlements was reduced by a third or more by the plague. Farm holdings, especially those on land that was marginal for arable agriculture, were being abandoned even before the first visitation of the plague in 1348, and, thereafter, this process accelerated, and in some settlements even the better lands remained untenanted. However, after the plague had passed, in most villages land was back in use within a generation. But the land was not unchanged. The new occupiers held it on easier terms and the uncultivated land, which had tumbled naturally to rough grass pasture, was often left in that state to provide grazing for larger flocks of sheep. At the beginning of the 15th century a new balance had been reached between the number of hands to work the land, the number of mouths to be fed, and the growing number of looms that needed to be supplied with wool in Coventry and other towns.

Examples of settlements shrinking almost to the point of desertion in this late 14th-century period include Fulbrook, which had half its tax abated in 1352 because there were so few inhabitants following the Black Death and where the manor house was in disrepair by 1392, and Billesley Trussell and

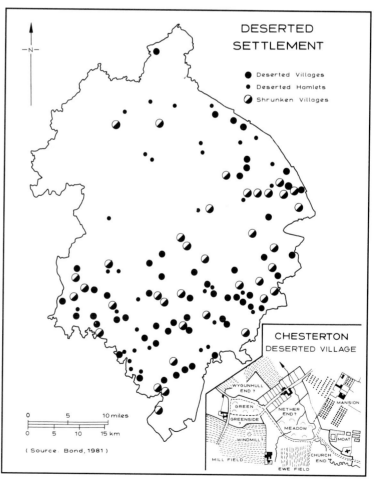

71 *Deserted settlement in Warwickshire*

Hodnell where there were only four households remaining in 1428. At Compton Verney and Kingston, in Chesterton parish, many holdings were untenanted and houses had fallen into disrepair by the 1390s. The surviving tenants were farming more land, consolidating their holdings from the open fields and beginning to convert to pasture farming. By 1437 at Kingston, and 1461 at Compton, there was virtually no arable cultivation. A similar process happened at Hatton-on-Avon, a formerly prosperous village on the Bishop of Worcester's estates, between Stratford and Hampton Lucy. Here it seems that many of the tenants who survived the plagues migrated elsewhere to take up land on easier terms than their conservative ecclesiastical overlord was prepared to offer. By 1386, 10 out of Hatton's 14 holdings were unoccupied. The village was totally deserted and the land turned over to pasture in the early 15th century.

By the 1480s the population had substantially recovered from the mid-14th-century decline. There were more men wanting land to farm, and there was thus an increasingly active land market among the peasant farmers. Similarly, lords who decided to rent out their former demesne land because there were no longer cultivators from whom they could demand labour services found ready tenants in grazier farmers specialising in sheep or cattle raising. These two groups, the peasant farmers, and the graziers, thus came into increasing conflict. For much of the second half of the 15th century wool prices were rising much more quickly than corn prices. There was little profit in corn, but the capital needed to invest in large-scale sheep rearing was beyond the means of peasant farmers. As a result more and more land was being turned over to pasture, although there were now people willing and able to farm these same lands. This continued for much of the first half of the 16th century when rising oxen and hide prices added cattle-raising to the various alternatives for profitably exploiting an estate. Social unrest was an inevitable consequence and government investigation and action followed.

One of the earliest protesters was John Rous, an historian and chantry priest at Guy's Cliff, near Warwick. In a history of the kings of England, written about 1486, he complains of 'the modern destruction of villages

72 *The deserted village site at Brookhampton. The grassed-over sunken street and rectangular house platforms and gardens of the former village can be clearly seen beyond the farmyard. The characteristic ridge and furrow of medieval open fields surround the village site.* (Cambridge University collection, copyright reserved)

bringing want to the State' and suggests that ' if such destruction took place in other parts of the kingdom as in Warwickshire it would be a danger to the whole country'. He follows with a list of some sixty places in the region around Warwick which he claims were 'destroyed' through the action of enclosures. They included Chesterton, where 79 inhabitants had been reduced to three; Charlecote, reduced from 42 to seven; and Compton Scorpion where a former village of 53 people had been totally deserted. In 1489 the government passed an 'Act against the pulling down of towns', while in 1515 another Act ordered all lands that had been converted to grass since 1488 to be returned to tillage. In 1517, and again in 1548, Commissions of Inquiry toured the Midlands taking evidence about recent enclosures and depopulation and protests continued throughout the 16th century culminating in the riots of 1607, when some 3,000 people gathered at Hillmorton to proclaim the manifesto of the 'Diggers of Warwickshire' against the decay of agriculture, high grain prices and the lack of employment.

74 *John Rous, 15th-century historian*

Capitalist Graziers

The men who carried out the depopulation of Feldon villages were overwhelmingly local men, men who had made their fortune in other places sometimes, but whose families still owned land in the area. In particular, they were men whose occupation brought them close to livestock farming; wool or cloth exporters, cloth-makers, butchers, and tanners were all closely involved. The ancestors of Henry Waver, the depopulator of Cestersover, had been lords there in the 13th century. He made his fortune in London as a draper and returned home to destroy the village, which had had 12 houses in 1385, and earlier still had been granted a market. Five hundred acres were enclosed as sheep pasture, and the manor house and chapel began to fall down. As early as 1437, the manor of Kingston had been leased to John Lichfelde, a Coventry butcher, and William Cope, who destroyed Wormleighton, was royal cofferer and had purchased it from the Crown in 1498. He sold it to his wife's family, the Spencers, who were great flock masters. William Willington, a stapler (wool merchant) bought Barcheston and depopulated it from 1509. Sir Edward Belknap had acquired, in 1473, half of Burton Dassett from his uncle. By 1498 he owned it all and proceeded to enclose 360 acres and destroyed 12 houses. By 1549, the enclosures had been doubled. Belknap was also responsible for the removal of Whitchurch village. Some of the wool merchants pastured enormous flocks over their enclosures. William Willington had somewhere between 12,000 and 18,000 sheep in the 1530s; Sir William Spencer and his mother between 7,000 and 10,000—yet later the Spencers became equally well-known as cattle farmers.

Inevitably, some of these men found themselves before the 1517 Commission of Inquiry, but were often able to defend themselves. John Spencer, who had purchased Wormleighton, claimed that the final depopulation of the village and the destruction of 12 houses and three

74 *Cowherd*

cottages had been the work of William Cope, the previous owner. He showed that he had built four new houses and a new manor house, and that the parish church was in better repair than for many years; while his new hedgerows provided much-needed timber. Sir Edward Belknap made similar claims for Burton Dassett saying there were then over thirty households in the parish and that depopulation was the fault of earlier owners.

The Spencers were perhaps the most successful of all the new breed of graziers in Warwickshire, and by the end of the 16th century had acquired lands in a contiguous block of no less than 14 parishes around Wormleighton, as well as others in Northamptonshire, the majority of which had been partly or totally depopulated. The earthworks of the village depopulated by Cope can still be seen on the slopes of the hill below Wormleighton church, with their house platforms, central green, fishponds, moated manor site, and channels for later water meadows. Spencer's new brick manor house survives in part beside the church and a 19th-century estate village stands where his new village was already building in the 16th century. To utilise properly his pastures so that they were not over-grazed, and to separate different kinds of stock, Spencer and other graziers planted substantial hedgerows 'double ditched and double hedged' with trees set between to provide much-needed timber. The larger graziers were also live-stock breeders. As Spencer was at pains to emphasise in 1517, his 'lyvyng ys and hathe byne by the brede of cattell in his pastures, for he ys neyther byer nor seller in common markettes as other grasyers be, but lyveth by his own brede of the same pastures and sold yt when it was fatt to the Citie of London'. 'Cattell' included sheep, cows and horses, and it was the first that was of greatest significance.

As many of this new breed of farmer made their fortunes they often sought to demonstrate their new station in life by building a mansion house and laying out a spacious deer park around it. This, too, was an action that could see the removal of settlements. At Fulbrook, the Duke of Bedford imparked much of the depleted arable of the parish in 1421 leaving only four households, and a century later the church, too, had gone. Fulbrook castle was itself later abandoned, and stone from it was taken to build another great house that supplanted a village, that of Compton Wynyates. Sir William Compton obtained royal permission to enclose 2,000 acres in 1510, and two years later enclosed a deer park which necessitated the eviction of some twenty householders. Work then began on his new mansion. At Weston, in Cherington parish, Henry Kebull, the Lord Mayor of London, was reported to have depopulated the village in 1509, destroying seven houses and a cottage, and enclosing 200 acres of arable land. By 1545, the manor was held by William Sheldon and he obtained licence to empark 300 acres as Weston Park. Sheldon is notable as having introduced tapestry weaving into England, and it is to him that we owe the beautiful tapestry map of Warwickshire that hangs in Warwick museum. The enclosure of Charlecote Park similarly saw the destruction of the village and the reduced population

75 *Late-medieval bridge, Bidford-on-Avon*

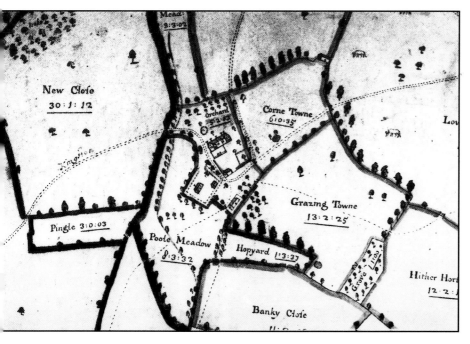

New Clofe
30:1:12

Mead:
3:3:02

Orchard

Corne Towne
6:0:35

Lo

Pingle 3:0:03

Grazing Towne
13:2:25

Poole Meadow
8:3:32

Hopyard 1:3:37

Grove 1:00

Banky Clofe
11:

Hither Hor
12:2:

76 *Map of Kingston, 1697. Kingston was one of the hamlets of the parish of Chesterton. Holdings were untenanted and cottages in disrepair by the 1390s. By 1437 the land was farmed as pasture. 'Corne Towne' and 'Grazing Towne' mark the site of the village, 'Poole Meadow' the site of a large fish-pond*

is indignantly recorded by John Rous. However, there was subsequent rebuilding here, as at Wormleighton, and also at Walton Deyville, where emparking in 1509 had destroyed the village and 40 people had been evicted, leaving only manor house and church.

Many of the places deserted and depopulated were among the smallest villages of the Feldon, but there were also a few very large settlements. Chesterton, for instance, had been a complex village with at least five separate medieval elements. Four manors are recorded in the Domesday Survey, and there were at least three areas of Romano-British settlement within the parish so it had been a populous place for many centuries. One hamlet was Kingston, or Little Chesterton, where now there is only Kingston Manor Farm. A large enclosure called 'Grazing Towne' on a map of 1697 marks the site of the deserted settlement and the earthworks of long-vanished buildings still cover the slopes. In Chesterton Magna, the large, now isolated, church was once surrounded by the long-gone cottages of Church End, while north of the church is the site of the moated manor and its associated fish-ponds. Around the extensive village green there were three more parts of the village: Greenide, Wygunhill End, and Nether End, the rectangular house platforms of the latter showing it to have been a regularly-planned addition. All were deserted, and today there remain only isolated farms and a few later farmworkers' cottages. Even the great 17th-century mansion of the Peytos, which took the place of the earlier manor house and stood in a well-planted park, has in its turn disappeared from the landscape.

77 *Leycester Hospital, Warwick*

The Dissolution of the Monasteries

Henry VIII's Dissolution of the Monasteries began in 1536 with the smaller houses. In Warwickshire, only six priories were dissolved in that year, but in 1537 work began on dismembering the estates of the larger monasteries, and in the following three years all the remaining institutions, including the friaries, were dissolved. They were followed by the chantries and religious guilds in the short reign of Edward VI. Most of the abbots, priors, monks and nuns were pensioned off, and within a few years buildings and property had been valued and then leased or sold to anyone prepared to enter the land market. Henry's commissioners could not always find things to complain of in the lives of monks and nuns to justify the dissolution. The abbess of Polesworth nunnery, Dame Alice Fitzherbert, for example was 'a very sadde, descrete, and relygyous woman' whilst the 12 nuns refused to abandon their habits or their highly regarded school.

Most of the great priory churches disappeared remarkably quickly— lead, glass, and well-cut stone finding their way into many a new-built town house or country mansion. The abbot's houses, grange farms, and mill buildings could be utilised directly, but churches survived only where towns-people or villagers made a determined effort to purchase them for parish use. The attempt to save St Mary's, Coventry, for the cathedral failed, but parts of Polesworth priory, Atherstone friary, and the Preceptory church of the Knights Templar at Temple Balsall were preserved as parish churches; a very small list indeed, and it includes nothing to match the surviving monastic churches of neighbouring counties, while in monastic ruins, too, the Warwickshire landscape is notably deficient.

At Coventry, the Corporation pleaded that the churches might be spared, but the Greyfriars church was razed, except for its steeple, and a merchant, John Hales, built himself a mansion on part of the site of the Whitefriars. The cathedral, too, and the domestic buildings of the priory were dismantled, the bishop's palace fell into ruins, and the see returned to Lichfield. Much of the land and many of the buildings were purchased by the Corporation and by local merchants and gentry. It was they who began to make provision for the poor and for education in the city once the hospitals and guilds had gone. Thomas Bond, William Ford and William Pisord founded almshouses for old people. John Hales founded the Free School, Sir Thomas White gave the Corporation a large sum of money to purchase priory lands, and Thomas Wheatley provided an endowment for Bablake Boys Hospital. The monopolies and restrictive practices of the Coventry guilds had slowly strangled the cloth trades in the 16th century, and the city fell upon hard times. In the 1520s more than 500 houses were standing empty and many families were moving elsewhere to find new opportunities for work. The Dissolution of the Monasteries added to these tribulations. John Leland describes the sur-viving glories of Coventry's many fine buildings in the mid-16th century, but he concluded sadly that 'the glory of the city decayethe'. It was to be another century before prosperity began to return to the city.

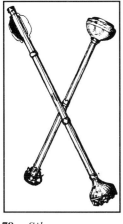

78 *Silver maces, Stratford-upon-Avon*

At Stratford, the dissolution of the College, and of the Guild of the Holy Cross, by Henry VIII gave an opportunity for the townspeople to petition the Crown for a Charter of Incorporation, obtained in 1555 but, in most of the smaller boroughs, local government remained vested in the manorial courts and parish vestry. Fire was a constant peril in towns through the medieval period and few escaped devastation. Once a fire began the timber-framed houses and thatched roofs burnt quickly. Stratford suffered a whole series of disastrous fires in the 1590s, in 1614, and again in 1641, which between them destroyed large areas of the town. As a result the Corporation began to demand the replacement of thatched roofs with tile, at least along the main streets, so that the majority of Stratford's 'Tudor' timbered buildings are, in fact, of early 17th-century origin.

79 *Tudor fire-fighting*

Country Houses

By the end of the 17th century Warwickshire was a county in which there was a large number of prosperous country estates, but which was not dominated by one great aristocratic family. There were members of the nobility living in the shire, but usually with no great ostentation. Some families had built up their estates over several centuries—the Shuckburghs had lived in the village of that name since the 12th century and became lords of the manor in 1540; and the Lucy family had lived at Charlecote for a similar length of time. The opportunities presented to some men of enterprise in the 15th and 16th centuries through enclosure and the rearing of livestock were further enhanced following the Dissolution of the Monasteries.

The Dissolution threw a very large quantity of land on to the market, and, though courtiers close to the Court in London often obtained huge estates, much was re-sold a few years later at a profit. Charles Brandon, Duke of Suffolk, for example, was granted the estates of Stoneleigh Abbey and Arbury Priory, but Stoneleigh was sold in 1561 to Sir Thomas Leigh, a Cheshire man who had been Lord Mayor in London in 1558, and Arbury was purchased by a lawyer, Edmund Anderson, who, in turn, exchanged it with the Newdigate family for a house nearer London. Some of these monastic estates were used to build new country houses, and often the stone from the demolished monasteries was used directly for the new house. Coombe, Stoneleigh, Arbury and Warwick Priory were all country houses of this kind, and tended to set new fashions. The older moats and crenellations of houses such as Coughton, Compton Wynyates, Beauchamps Court and Maxstoke were abandoned for a new expansiveness with large windows, fine rooms, extensive gardens and the house set four-square in the landscape. Several Warwickshire houses entertained Tudor monarchs. Kenilworth saw Elizabeth I several times, and each time Robert Dudley sought to outdo rivals in the splendour of his reception, while Sir Thomas Lucy also entertained Elizabeth in 1572, at Charlecote. Charlecote was one of the 'new' mansions of the age, rebuilt in 1558 with a characteristic 'E' plan, but there are none of the great Tudor and Stuart mansions to match those of neighbouring Northamptonshire. Perhaps the largest is Aston Hall, in Birmingham, built for Sir Thomas Holte between 1618 and 1630. The Holtes had been lords of the manor since the 15th century.

Inevitably, in the rapidly changing political circumstances of the 16th and 17th centuries, some families suffered as well. The Duke of Suffolk's Brandon Castle was deserted and eventually demolished following their disgrace, as was Mount Grevill, the uncompleted home of Ludovic Grevill at Milcote, near Straford. At Coughton Court, the home of the Throckmorton family from 1409, that family's continued adherence to Roman Catholicism meant that the house had to be adapted to hide priests and vestments during periods of religious persecution. In 1583, the Throckmortons had been at the head of a plot to depose Elizabeth I in favour of Mary, Queen of Scots, and as late as 1688 the house was sacked by an anti-Catholic mob from nearby Alcester.

Changing Standards of Living

It is only from the middle of the 16th century that there is sufficient evidence to assess the ways in which the living standards of the majority of the population changed. At that time there was probably a four-tier social structure in the county. At the top were the aristocracy living in substantial brick- or stone-built mansions in considerable luxury; then came the gentry, wealthy yeomen, and many rectors who lived mostly in comparatively comfortable and spacious houses with kitchens, parlours and upstairs bedrooms; then other yeomen, craftsmen and more prosperous husbandmen who possessed houses with a hall and bed-chamber and perhaps a kitchen, but no upper floor rooms, and at the bottom of the scale were the labourers and smallholders who lived in simple one- or two-roomed hovels with very few facilities indeed. In the majority of cottages furnishings were spartan. William Orme of Bickenhill had a two-roomed cottage in 1557; the 'Chamber' had 'bedsteddes iii' with their coverings, and three chests for storage together with some of his tools, including a 'dungforke'! In the 'Hall' was a board table, 'benche formes ii', 'chers ii' and the hearth with its 'pothockes & pothangles'.

Most of these cottages were built with 'crucks': pairs of timbers supporting the walls and rafters of each bay and rising from floor to roof ridge. Surviving examples in Warwickshire date from the late 14th to the early 16th century. No less than six are to be found in Stoneleigh, four of which are of three bays and two of two bays. Two of these houses have recently been dated dendrochronologically to the late 15th century. In the mid-16th century they were occupied by people of very different status. In one lived John and Elizabeth Jones, who were ale brewers and sellers, a lowly cottager occupation. In 1585 he was fined 1s. for allowing cards to be played in his house and was frequently presented at the manor court for contravening the assize of beer. By contrast, Godfrey Parton, who lived in one of the three-bay crucks in the 1550s was a much more well-to-do farmer. His two chambers (bedrooms) contained four beds (two with feather matTresses), bolsters, blankets, coverlets and '8 pere of herden shetes' and '2 pere of flaxon schettes'.

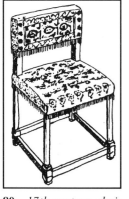

80 *17th-century chair at Aston Hall*

One of these chambers must have been in the roof since the common pattern was for rooms and bays to correspond, so that a three-bay cottage provided a room to live in (the hall), a room to cook in (the kitchen), and a room to sleep in (the parlour or chamber). Where there were only two rooms the hall and kitchen were combined.

81 Four-poster bed, Compton Wynyates

With the general increase in prosperity during Elizabeth's reign many country dwellers were able to improve their living conditions. Houses were extended, first with kitchens if there was none previously, which were sometimes built separate from the main dwelling to diminish the risk of fire, and subsequently with additional 'chambers' which allowed family members to sleep in separate rooms. By the end of the 16th century many houses had been extended further, or completely rebuilt, with rooms on the first floor reached by an interior staircase. Brick chimney stacks were also being added at this time to replace open hearths, and, at least in north-east Warwickshire, allowed coal to be used as a domestic fuel. Increasingly, too, window glass was fitted in the houses of the better-off yeomen, but was treated as an item that could be removed with the furniture. Christopher Kirkland, the vicar of Rowington in 1584, had glass in his hall, parlour, study, and two chamber windows as well as wainscot panelling in the parlour; all of which belonged to him personally and not to the vicarage.

The period 1570-1640 has been characterised as that of 'The Great Rebuilding' of rural England as living standards rose and farming prospered. This seems true in much of north Warwickshire but less so in the south. Timber framing and thatch roofs were still the norm but the houses of yeoman farmers and the more prosperous husbandmen were almost always of two floors by 1620 and had a multiplicity of bedrooms, storage rooms (for wool or cheese, for example), and specialised service rooms, especially butteries, dairies and brewhouses.

In the later 17th century, living conditions continued to improve, though for most social classes rather more slowly than in the previous century. For those who had all they needed in terms of rooms, attention turned to embellishments such as murals and wainscotting, while furniture was of a much higher standard, often with morticed and tenoned joints. Life was also becoming softer and more comfortable for those outside the poorest classes. By the 1640s, wealthier farmers were buying expensive clothes and other personal goods and their houses contained a wealth of 'soft' furnishings. John Muston, of Horeston Grange near Nuneaton, had 19 hempen and 10 flaxen napkins, seven pairs of coarse sheets, four pairs of 'better' sheets and five pillowcases in one chamber. In the second half of the century, card tables, curtained beds, desks, carpets, looking-glasses, brass and pewter were found in many houses. It was not unusual to find up to 50 per cent of a person's assessed wealth could be classified under items bought for personal use rather than being the tools of his trade or his farm equipment. By the early 18th century less than 10 per cent of most villagers still lived in one-roomed houses, and many labourers had possessions sufficient to make a will. In 1747 an Ilmington man had an estate valued at £4 15s. 0d. and his

82 Mayor's state chair, Coventry

goods included a spade, axe, four pewter dishes, a dozen trenchers (wooden dishes), six chairs, two tables, a fire grate, and a grain tub.

Piety and Puritans

The Reformation brought great changes to parish churches in the mid-16th century. The dissolution of the chantries saw the demolition of chantry chapels whilst Lutheran doctrines against all forms of idolatry saw medieval rood screens pulled down, statues smashed and wall paintings whitewashed whilst the Book of Common Prayer was introduced to order services. Some things were replaced during Mary's reign in the 1550s, but Elizabeth's accession in 1559 established the Church of England. However, in Warwickshire, there remained a significant Roman Catholic presence. It was strongest in the west of the county where many of the wealthiest members of the gentry class were Catholics. They included the Smiths of Wootton Wawen, the Sheldons of Weston, the Middlemores of Edgbaston and the Throckmortons of Coughton. The villages where the houses of these Catholic families were located also tended to have large numbers of 'recusants', as Catholics were called. At all levels, they were a cohesive social group with strong marriage and social ties and this was emphasised at times of persecution. Brailes, where the Sheldons had a second house, was another centre of recusancy and 57 Catholics are listed as living there in 1628.

83   *Coughton Court*

At the other end of the spectrum there was also a staunch Protestant or Puritan element in Warwickshire. The leaders and protectors of this group in Elizabethan Warwickshire were Ambrose Dudley, Earl of Warwick and his brother Robert, Earl of Leicester. They looked to further reformation of the Church and conferences of local ministers were held to this end in Coventry and at Southam. In the years leading up to the Civil War, Warwick Castle continued to offer sanctuary for Puritan ministers as the second Lord Brooke was a sympathizer, as were Sir Thomas and Lady Alice Lucy at Charlecote.

The period of the Commonwealth brought Presbyterianism to the fore but the majority of ministers in Warwickshire wanted a reformed, Calvinist national church, not an increasingly divided set of independent congregations. The main towns of Birmingham and Coventry seem to have accepted this view but there were radical congregations in other towns. There was an Independent congregation led by James Cooke in Warwick through the 1650s, and there were Particular Baptists in Coventry, Warwick and Alcester. They believed in strict separatism from people of other beliefs whilst women in the congregation could testify but could not teach since this would 'be usurping of authority over the man'. Radical preachers were active in Henley-in-Arden, Monks Kirby and Long Lawford. The 1650s also saw the beginnings of the Quakers' public ministry. George Fox was holding well-attended meetings in north and north-east Warwickshire, especially at Baddesley Ensor, and along the Oxfordshire border where Quaker groups are known in Ettington, Gaydon, Radway and Brailes. In the years leading o the Restoration, Quaker meetings were frequently broken up whilst many individuals were imprisoned for non-payment of tithes. For the majority of people, however, the liturgy of the Book of Common Prayer and the regular rhythm of the Christian festivals remained unsuppressed.

The Civil War

From the beginning, Warwickshire found itself at the centre of the conflict between king and parliament; between roundhead and cavalier. This was partly because it stood on the geographical divide between the generally economically advanced south and east, with mostly parliamentary sympathies, and the less developed pastoral economies of the north and west, with more royalist sympathies. But it was partly, too, the deep religious divisions long apparent in the county and the presence of energetic and committed leaders in the form of Lord Brooke of Warwick Castle and the Earl of Northampton at Compton Wynyates. Lord Brooke was a radical and uncompromising puritan; the earl a loyal court favourite of the king. Finally, there was the county's position astride the major road network linking the key towns of Oxford and Worcester for the royalists; Coventry, Warwick and London for the parliamentarians. The southern part of Warwickshire was therefore subjected to constant military and supply movements throughout the period of the war, so that villages, and the ordinary people living in them, could not ignore what was taking place on the national stage.

The drift to war began with musters of all males aged 16 to 60 in the summer of 1642. Both king and parliament sent out Warrants for this purpose to constables and church-wardens, and local men then had to report fully-armed and with carts and supplies for military training. Through June and July there were musters for parliament, organised by Lord Brooke, at Stratford, Warwick, Coleshill and Coventry, and for the king, organised by the Earl of Northampton, at Southam, Stratford, Warwick and Coleshill. For many men it was a day's journey to the muster and most were tired, armed only with hedgebills or clubs, bored at the waiting and lack of organisation and therefore happy to fraternise in the streets and taverns of the towns, rather than stand about on the heath or meadows where the muster was properly held. Other, more local, musters were held on their estates by local magnates. There are records of one at Winderton in Brailes parish, for example. At the same time, Lord Brooke was busy strengthening the defences of his castle at Warwick, moving the county arms from Coventry into the castle and taking 'men ynto Warwick Castle for the defence of the magasyn there' to the general alarm of moderate opinion. However, he was unable to move the Banbury magazine to Warwick when his waggon train of arms was intercepted on Warmington Hill by a superior force of Northampton's men. He was forced to return it to Banbury after a day of tense negotiation. A month later the royalists had become more organised and succeeded in removing the arms to Compton Wynyates. Local puritans were threatened, especially the clergy; James Nalton was attacked in his church at Rugby and Lord Dunsmore succeeded in robbing 'our towne of ther armes' according to Richard Newton.

At the beginning of August 1642, siege was laid to Warwick Castle by the Earl of Northampton. The castle was in the charge of Sir Edward Peto of Chesterton and had a garrison of perhaps 300 armed men 'out of oure towne of Alcester and from Stradford and from Brummychum side, and all the Country over'. The siege began with the high drama of William Dugdale, clad in his red and gold robes as King's herald, summoning Sir Edward to surrender and declaring him traitor on his refusal. The arms available to the besiegers were completely inadequate for the task of taking the carefully prepared castle and for much of the time the royalists vented their frustration on the surrounding countryside and the town. Subsequent reports speak of them daily committing 'great spoile and outrage against any that seem well affected to the Parliament' and 'pillaging in the little townes; they steale Horse, Cowes, Sheepe, Cloathes and Victualls'. They also broke the pale of Wedgnock Park and killed as many of the deer as they could. A royalist cannon was placed on the tower of St Mary's church; a parliamentary cannon ball demolished one of the pinnacles of the tower; there was some damage to houses in West Street; a butcher was shot dead taunting the castle defenders.

By mid-August Lord Brooke was marching to relieve his castle at the head of a large force from London, whilst the king moved from York to Nottingham. Somewhere near Budbrooke, on 18 August, two equally matched armies of between five and six thousand horse and foot soldiers came face to face with much drum-beating, threats and negotiation. On this occasion they marched away from each other, but the siege was lifted and the war was about to begin. The first real fighting between the two armies took place five days later in the fields between Long Itchington and Southam. The royalists came off worse and the fields were 'much besprinkled with blood'. Lord Brooke gave money to enable the dead to be carried to Southam church for burial; local residents were compelled to quarter troops and many lost possessions and food to ill-disciplined looting.

Two months later, the first great battle of the war, Edgehill, was to take place. The Earl of Essex, as supreme parliamentary commander, left London in early September. On 20 September a great rally of parliamentary forces took place on Dunsmore Heath. Almost every village in east and central Warwickshire was forced to accept its quota of soldiers for quartering as the army moved across the county towards Worcester. Royalist houses were ransacked, including Coughton Court where pictures and 'popish Bookes' were burnt or thrown into the moat and feather beds maliciously emptied round the house. After three weeks in Worcester, the parliamentary army found the king had moved east from Shrewsbury and he held a great rally of troops on 18 October on Meriden Heath, symbolically the centre of his kingdom. Next day, the king's army began to march south for London as Essex's army began, once more, the trek across Warwickshire's muddy lanes and highways. Once again, almost every community in the county found

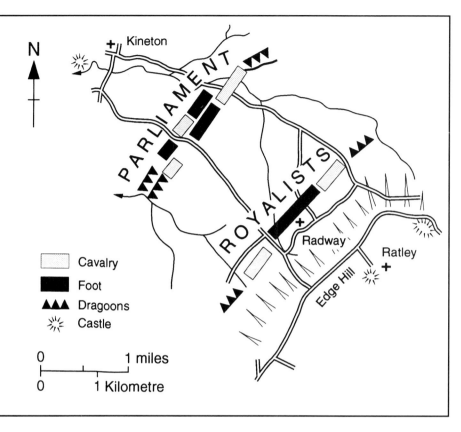

84 *The battle of Edgehill*

tself obliged to supply food, horses and accommodation to the soldiery of he slow-moving armies.

The king's baggage train was looted by Captain John Bridges and the Warwick Castle garrison as it headed for Southam and a proposed attack on Banbury. On 22 October the king learnt that the parliamentary army was at Kineton, also marching to Banbury, and he therefore ordered his army to turn and occupy the commanding heights of Edge Hill. By daybreak, Prince Rupert had deployed his cavalry on the scarp and the foot-soldiers were assembled by midday. The Earl of Essex was on his way to church in Kineton when the alarm was raised that the royalist army was advancing only three miles away. The Sunday morning was 'as fair a day as that season of the year could yield'. King Charles rode amongst his troops making a brief rallying speech and Prince Rupert led a cavalry charge on the right flank, Lord Wilmot on the left. It was brilliantly successful but the cavalry was not easily reformed after this first charge. A prolonged hand-to-hand battle then ensued between the two infantry groups lasting until nightfall when the exhausted armies camped out on the battlefield amongst the dead and dying. Total casualties are usually reckoned at about 3,000 men. Next day, the Earl of Essex retreated to the stronghold at Warwick, leaving Banbury

at the mercy of the king and the road to London wide open. This first se
battle of the Civil War left King Charles with the strategic advantage.

Edge Hill was the principal battle of the Civil War in Warwickshire, but
the shire continued to suffer from the passage of armies and smaller
skirmishes throughout the following decade of intermittent strife. The
inhabitants of agricultural villages found their possessions stolen or
requisitioned, market towns were occasionally occupied by troops; country
houses were vandalised, and churches wrecked. Coughton Court was
bombarded and sacked by Royalist troops in 1644 after it had been occupied
by a force of Parliamentarians. Compton Wynyates was another house badly
damaged during the Civil War, again after a siege in 1644. When it was
restored to the Earl of Northampton two years later, he had to pay a fine
of £20,000, fill in the moat around the house, and destroy the fortifications.
Sir Thomas Holte of Aston Hall faced a similar fine after 40 royalist soldiers
had vainly endeavoured to defend the house against a parliamentary force
of more than a thousand men. In contrast, Warwick Castle, despite being
garrisoned for much of the Commonwealth period, was returned to Lord
Brooke relatively unscathed. At Kenilworth the parliamentary garrison were
ordered to make the castle untenable in 1649, though not to damage the
living quarters. Part of the walls of the keep and base court were accordingly
demolished, and the great lake was drained. The castle was never again to
be occupied and it slowly deteriorated to a picturesque ruin.

VII *Warwick Castle. The prospect of the domestic range and great eastern towers and gatehouse of Warwick Castle seen from the bridge over the Avon, built in 1793, is one of the great views of England. The ruins of the medieval Great Bridge can be seen below the castle.*

VIII *The West Gate, Chapel of St James and Lord Leycester's Hospital, Warwick. The gate and chapel were rebuilt in the late 14th century, probably when the chapel was given to the Guild of St George. The 15th-century quadrangle of the Guild was converted into a hospital in 1571 by Robert Dudley, Earl of Leicester.*

IX *Cruck house, Stoneleigh. There are six cruck-built houses in Stoneleigh village. This example is dated by dendrochronology to the late 15th century. The three bays contained a hall, with central open fireplace, and a parlour. The pair of cruck timbers support the roof ridge at each end.*

X *Warmington village. Warmington lies on the Cotswold scarp close to Edge Hill. It is built around a triangular green complete with a pond. The lovely houses are built of Horton stone and the Manor House of c.1600 stands fronting the green, like the well-built cottages, a few of which are even older. The church stands apart on the hill-top.*

7

Change in the Countryside, 1660-1900

Lords and the Landscape

Following the Restoration of Charles II there was a spate of country house building and park planting, both in Warwickshire and nationally. In Warwickshire the biggest houses were Coombe Abbey, which was extensively reconstructed by the Earl of Craven in the 1680s, and Ragley Hall, built by Lord Conway, Secretary of State to Charles II. Ragley is one of the largest and finest houses in Warwickshire and was built in the 1670s after Lord Conway had received an earldom, though it has subsequently been altered several times. The gardens were equally magnificent with a formal layout of parterres, flower beds, clipped trees and hedges, and gravel paths surrounding the house. Beyond was a large wooded park with avenues leading from the gardens. Today, these intricate garden layouts are known only from contemporary engravings. There were gardens on a similar scale at Newnham Paddox, Four Oaks Hall and Weston, while the well-known painting of Charlecote in 1696 shows Dutch influence with a long canal an important feature of the gardens. The smaller houses also had their well-tended gardens, normally behind warm brick walls from which little pavilions provided a look-out: those in the National Trust gardens at Packwood are good examples. The yew garden at Packwood is also of 17th-century origin, and is an unusual survival from this period. The greatest gardeners of the late 17th century were George London and Henry Wise. The latter purchased Warwick Priory for his retirement and laid out a small formal garden around the Tudor house.

85 *Topiary at Compton Wynyates*

The sort of men investing in new estates included merchants and lawyers from London, such as Sir Henry Parker, the builder of Honington Hall, and Ambrose Holbech, who built Farnborough Hall. Few Warwickshire families took advantage of the Hanoverian succession in 1714 to increase their wealth, and most remained staunch Tories throughout the 18th century. Country house building in the 18th century was therefore financed through estate improvement, through advantageous marriages, and, increasingly, on the basis of industrial wealth. Sir Roger Newdigate's rebuilding of Arbury Hall, for example, was facilitated by the exploitation of the coal on his estate which nearly doubled the estate income in the second half of the 18th century. Elmdon Hall was built by Isaac Spooner, a Birmingham banker and one of the leading citizens of the day, while Packington Hall was rebuilt when the third Earl of Aylesford chose to live there, his mother's home, rather than at

86 *Oval pavilion, Farnborough Hall*

81

87 *Ragley Hall, 1707. Ragley was built in the 1670s for Lord Conway, Secretary of State to Charles II. The ornate gardens with parterres, fountains, clipped trees and avenues leading out to the park were swept away by 'Capability' Brown in the 1760s*

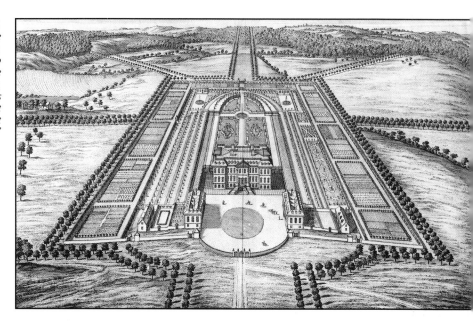

88 *Ragley Hall, 1969. Brown's landscape gardens with lawns, clumps of trees and a serpentine lake is the basis of the present park. However, there is also a Victorian shrub garden and a modern formal garden and avenue. Stable block and portico were added in 1750-80*

the family seat in Surrey. These houses were among the finest of the 18th century, together with Compton Verney, designed by Robert Adam in 1760-5, and the earlier Newbold Revel, designed by Francis Smith, the well-known Warwick architect-builder. Arbury is especially noted for its Gothic Revival architecture, probably the designs of Sanderson Miller, the squire-architect of Radway Grange in the Cotswold fringe of south Warwickshire. Miller was an important figure, too, in the changing attitude to garden design which saw the intricate Dutch gardens of the 17th century eventually swept away in favour of a naturalistic sweep of lawn with trees and lakes. Another early proponent of the new style was Joseph Addison, who purchased Bilton Hall, near Rugby, in 1711, and laid out the gardens there.

The greatest exponent of the landscape garden was Lancelot 'Capability' Brown, and a number of Warwickshire landowners commissioned him to lay out their parks anew. Lord Brooke provided one of his earliest commissions at Warwick Castle, and Brown's plans were instrumental in encouraging the first Earl of Warwick to proceed with a scheme that was to continue for 50 years, and eventually nearly bankrupted the estate. Briefly, large numbers of houses in the town were demolished, roads closed, a new bridge over the Avon provided, a new stable block built, and thousands of trees planted in order to provide the rural scenery that was an essential attribute to any great country house. Brown also worked at Coombe Abbey (where much of the garden was subsequently re-modelled in the 19th century by William Nesfield), at Charlecote, and at Compton Verney, all in the 1760s, and at Edgbaston in the mid-1770s. At Compton Verney he was also involved in architectural work providing designs for a chapel and orangery. Brown was especially admired for his lakes, and his Warwickshire commissions at Coombe and Compton Verney contain two of his most beautiful stretches of naturalised water. The other great English landscape gardener, Humphry Repton, who worked in the late 18th and early 19th centuries, had only one commission in Warwickshire—at Moseley Hall in Birmingham, where a part of his garden is now a private park surrounded by Edwardian houses.

By the end of the 18th century many of the smaller manor houses of the 17th century had been downgraded to farms, as their owners had either fallen on hard times, or had moved up the social scale and built themselves grand new houses. Generally, it was the former process, since the divisions between the nobility and lesser gentry widened as the century progressed. By 1800, there were far fewer country seats with their

89 *Compton Verney house*

90 *The location of parks and great houses*

91 *Perrott's folly, Edgbaston, 1756*

landscape parks and classical mansions than there had been in 1700, while the estates which supported this highest echelon of society were much larger. Lord Leigh had over 20,000 acres in the Stoneleigh estate, and there were similar-sized estates supporting the Marquess of Hertford at Ragley and the Earl of Warwick at Warwick Castle. Many of these families also held land elsewhere, including a town house in London. Throughout the period the land-owning families dominated the social, economic and political life of the county. The social round centred on Warwick in the 18th century with the Quarter Sessions, Assembly Rooms, Shire Hall and racecourse. One or two great houses also became centres of society in their own right for short periods, most notably Barrels Park, near Oldberrow, where Lady Luxborough presided over a literary circle in the period 1739-56 that included William Shenstone, Somerville, and Richard Graves.

Enclosing the Fields

The enclosing of open-field arable lands by landowners went on continuously from the 14th century, accompanied in many parishes by the desertion of villages and the conversion of land from arable to pasture. In the 16th and early 17th centuries this resulted in increasingly voluble social protest and successive government enquiries. However, there was relatively little action and the enclosure of open land continued apace through the 17th century. In order to ensure the legality of such private enclosure of land, especially when more than one owner was involved, agreements were sometimes enrolled in Quarter Sessions records or in the Chancery court in London, and such agreements provide some record of the progress of 17th-century enclosure. In 1614-18 the lord of Welcome, near Stratford, William Combe, proposed enclosure, but he was opposed in the Assizes, and subsequently by a petition to the Privy Council, by Thomas Greene, and no less than William Shakespeare, who were joint lessees of the tithes. They were successful and Welcome remained open. However, at Long Itchington at least 13 of the 30 yardlands of the open fields had been enclosed by 1636 and, at Wootton Wawen, Sir Charles Smith had 'inclosed parte of the Common field ... and also inclosed a wast called millane towards Henley by estimation forescore acres or there aboutes' in 1640, and his father had enclosed a further 300 acres 17 years previously.

Clearly such piecemeal actions were not necessarily the most efficient means of enclosing and there was a demand for an Act of Parliament to ease the process. A Bill of this kind was rejected in 1664, and, thereafter, the same ends were pursued by means of a series of private Acts each relating only to one or two parishes. Only a few such Acts were presented before 1700, but by 1760 more than 250 had been passed and some 33 (12 per cent) related to Warwickshire, the largest number for any single county. Warwickshire was in the forefront, therefore, of the parliamentary enclosure movement.

There were four main objects behind such enclosures. First, enclosure made for more efficient arable farming by consolidating farm units. This in

92 *Chesterton windmill*

its turn often encouraged the adoption of convertible husbandry, a better balance between arable and pasture, and the improvement of soil fertility. The second objective was to convert land to more profitable use. Thus, exhausted arable land might be rendered more profitable when laid down to grass, while to the landowner enclosed farmland could be let at higher rents than open land. Thirdly, the enclosure of commons and wastes increased the area under cultivation and the elimination of fallow fields substantially increased cultivable land within any one year. Finally, most enclosures disposed of tithes within the parish, the tithe holder gaining a portion of the land in lieu, and brought greater order and convenience to the road and footpath network. Inevitably there were difficulties and disadvantages as well, especially to those holding only tiny quantities of land and common rights. Before enclosure such smallholders were just able to survive. Afterwards, they were unable to afford the costs of enclosure and normally sold their holding to become landless labourers.

93 *Mouldboard plough*

Once the principal landowners in a parish decided upon enclosure, commissioners were appointed by Parliament to enquire into the holdings and common rights in the parish and to survey the parish. The expenses of the commissioners and surveyor, as well as the legal fees for the Act, had to be borne by the petitioners. To these costs had to be added those of laying out the new roads and paths on the ground and the cost of fencing or hedging the outer boundaries of the new holdings. The capital needed to finance enclosure was therefore considerable and it is not surprising to find that in Warwickshire, as elsewhere, it was the larger landowners who were in the forefront of the movement to enclose. Costs rose as the 18th century progressed. In the first half of the century the cost averaged about eleven shillings an acre. By the 1780s this had risen to 19 shillings an acre, and in the 1790s it had almost doubled to 34 shillings an acre. In part, this was because the parishes enclosed first were those where costs were likely to be low since agricultural prices generally were relatively depressed until the 1790s. Thereafter, as prices rose, particularly through the 1790s and the Napoleonic Wars, the most problematic parishes—those with a diversity of landowners, for example—were also enclosed. In 1801, the first of a number of General Inclosure Acts made the whole process rather easier.

Some 175 Enclosure Acts relate to Warwickshire, two-thirds of which included open-field arable. The first, Lighthorne, was passed in 1720 and the last, Stoke Common, in 1886. The last enclosure making reference to open-field land was that for Langley in 1831-5 and this included a mere 51 acres, mostly in scattered parcels. By contrast, some of the 18th-century Acts enclosed several thousand acres of open-field land. Prior's Marston, for example, enclosed in 1758, possessed over 3,300 acres of open fields; Southam (1761) over 2,000 acres; Napton (1778) over 3,600 acres; and Brailes (1787) 3,500 acres. These parishes are all in the Feldon, of course, and in many townships in this region almost the whole area of the parish remained to be enclosed.

94 *Kinwarton parish,*
1752-1886

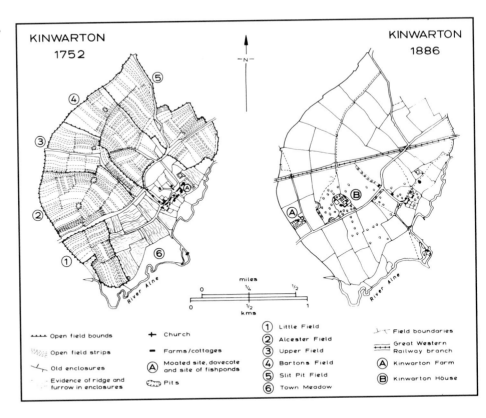

In contrast, in Arden townships open-field areas were small and the enclosure of waste, heath and common was much more significant. This sort of enclosure took place in the early 19th century. The first parishes to enclose were generally those in the Avon valley—Wellesbourne, Newbold Pacy, Bubbenhall, Brinklow, and Churchover, for example, where agricultural practices were already quite advanced and where soils were productive. By the 1770s the majority of the heavy clay soil parishes of Feldon were being enclosed and it was only thereafter that Cotswold fringe parishes and townships in the Arden and North Warwickshire regions began to be enclosed. Some parishes were enclosed in groups, notably those within the lordship of a single landowner. Once he had decided upon the efficacy of enclosure it normally took less than a decade for the majority of his estates to be enclosed and this effect was not constrained by county boundaries; the Spencer lands stretch across into Warwickshire from Northamptonshire; the Dukes of Buccleuch had extensive east Warwickshire estates, though their seats were all elsewhere, while some landowners were almost entirely absentee, as at Grandborough where the Award of 1766 divides the lands between Charles Isham and Edward Lockwood of Northamptonshire, John Clarke and Robert Brown of the City of London, and, the sole Warwickshire man, 'Edward Hewitt of Grandburrow, weaver'.

Once the enclosure Award had been made by the Commissioners to the satisfaction of all involved, work began on reorganising the parish. Roads were often straightened and drainage ditches provided, and they were enclosed between boundary hedges or walls to give a fixed width. Main highways were normally forty to fifty feet wide and lesser routes rather narrower. In Norton Lindsey, for example, enclosed in 1809, the Warwick road was 40ft. wide, the lanes to Snitterfield and Hatton 30ft. wide, a bridleway to Sherborne 15ft. wide, and footpaths 6ft. wide. The roads had a gravel surface in the centre and the verges provided some small substitute for the lost common grazings of the cottagers.

The farms themselves also needed reorganising, once the initial expense of enclosing had been catered for, since open-field farms were concentrated in the villages. The Commissioners only rarely created wedge-shaped new holdings focusing on the village and some holdings were therefore at a distance from the settlement. In the decade following the enclosure these landowners would normally move their farm from the village to the centre of their new holding. A common feature of the south Warwickshire land-scape is the isolated, brick-built farm with a tiled roof, early 19th-century in origin and linked to the nearest lane by its own trackway. This is especially noticeable in the extreme south where local limestone and marlstone is used in the villages and contrasts markedly with the brick farmhouses in the fields. Such farms also have distinctive names: Field House, North Field Farm, Grandborough Fields Farm, New Fields Farm, and many others of this type.

The landscape of parishes enclosed by Parliamentary Act is generally very orderly. Besides the straight roads and the neat Georgian farmhouses, the fields, too, are laid out in rectangular blocks. Once the ring fence or hedge had been completed it was up to the landowner to sub-divide his allotment as he saw fit, but the normal pattern was of large regular fields of between 10 and 20 acres in size. The hedgerows that divided the fields were usually hawthorn, though occasionally other species were deliberately intermingled to provide variety. Standard trees were planted every dozen yards along the hedge, especially if the land was to be laid down to pasture, so that as these trees matured the Feldon landscape viewed from the Dassett Hills or Edge Hill was a remarkably well-wooded countryside; an impression given further credence when 19th-century farmers planted fox and game coverts in the angles of many fields. The post-war combination of arable farming and the depredations of elm disease has only recently destroyed this impression.

The 19th-century waste and heathland enclosures of north Warwickshire created a very similar landscape, except that it was perhaps even more regular, as the surveyors were working with a clean sheet. Straight roads and rectangular fields form a great swathe from Temple Balsall to Shrewley as a result of the enclosure of 1796, and similarly at Coleshill Heath and Elmdon Heath. Heath names are common in Birmingham and these places were mostly open until the mid-19th century. Birmingham Heath was enclosed

95 *Farmhand with scythe*

96 *Longhorn Warwickshire bullock*

97 *Rickyard at Great Alne, 1890. A busy farmyard scene at harvest time. In the background sheaves are unloaded for threshing in the steam-powered threshing machine. The thatched rick in the centre is raised on staddle stones and there is a traditional bowed waggon*

in 1798 and its 400 acres provided land for prison, workhouse and lunatic asylum. There were other open areas at Shirley Heath, Balsall Heath, Wake Green, Billesley Common, and Perry Barr Common, which were all subsequently enclosed and much of their area was used for building.

Farming Systems

Agricultural practices naturally varied from place to place in the county, and also through time. The Feldon lands of south Warwickshire which Leland had described as 'very plentiful of corne' were already being converted to pastures by the early 18th century. Once the lands had been enclosed, pastures followed quickly and by 1800 Warwickshire was 'almost throughout a dairying county'. Mixed farming, with above average quantity of grazing lands, predominated in the north-west and south and there was rather more arable in the Avon valley and the north. The Feldon soils are largely intractable Lower Lias clay; very heavy, retentive of moisture and slow to warm up in the Spring. Traditionally, this was grain-growing country, but it also provided exceptionally rich grazing land when well managed. Following the Tudor and 18th-century enclosures it remained a pastoral

region until the 1950s when it was once again ploughed up for barley cropping.

Drainage was important on these heavy soils and in some areas poor grass and rushes had been allowed to infest the furrows of the heavily ridged land by the early 19th century so that they remained water-logged for much of the year. Joseph Elkington, a farmer of Princethorpe, had attracted much attention in the mid-18th century by developing new methods of under-draining these heavy lands, but it was really not until the advent of cheap tile drains in the mid-19th century that these problems were resolved. Properly constructed water meadows were not especially common in Warwickshire though they are recorded in the lower Stour valley and in the Tame valley below Aston. They were still in use in this latter area in the first half of the 19th century and since much of the sewage effluent from Birmingham found its way into the Tame and Rea these waters had excellent fertilising properties.

98 *The improved Tamworth pig*

On the Arden plateau lands the Mercian Mudstone soils were somewhat lighter because of overlying glacial drift. A characteristic form of improvement in the 17th and 18th centuries in the region was the use of marl. The slightly calcareous marl was dug from pits in the corner of fields and spread over the surface to improve the lime content and tilth of the glacial gravels. Marling is documented as early as 1250, but had ceased by the early 19th century to be replaced by liming. The remnant marl pits are now usually water-filled and a very characteristic feature of north-west Warwickshire.

Arable crops were grown in rotations and though the use of new rotational practices is a characteristic of agricultural improvement all over England in the 18th century, experiments on the open-field lands were also taking place rather earlier. It is probably for this reason that the multiple-field systems of the Avon Valley were introduced in the 16th and 17th centuries, and the four-field systems elsewhere. In the south, traditional rotations involved wheat, barley, beans and oats, with fallow remaining the principal means of 'cleaning' the soil, while in the north and the Avon valley turnips were increasingly used. By the later 18th century quite complex rotations were in use: wheat was succeeded by peas or vetches, then barley, then clover or turnips, and barley again. The light, warm soils of the gravel terraces of the Avon valley were the most important arable farming region throughout the 18th and 19th centuries, though farmers were not always the most efficient.

Improved livestock breeding was an important factor in the 18th-century agricultural revolution, and here Warwickshire's farmers were of some significance nationally, especially once open fields had been enclosed and animals no longer had to be mixed with other herds and flocks on the common grazings. Improvements in sheep breeds are especially associated with Robert Bakewell's New Leicester breed. These were already being raised by the end of the 18th century in south Warwickshire, along the Cotswold fringe, around Rugby and along the borders with Leicestershire, and farmers in these areas were experimenting with further cross-breeding. The Earl of Aylesford, at Packington, was a great agricultural innovator and was using

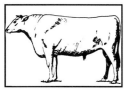

99 *18th-century improved Shorthorn*

both Wiltshire breeds and Spanish Merinos on his farms in the early 19th century. Another farmer experimenting with the fine-woolled Merinos was Thomas Jackson of Alveston Pastures, near Stratford, who had a flock of 600, while Lord Hood was using South Downs on his estates near Coventry as they were well adapted to folding.

Cattle raising in the 18th century changed in emphasis from dairy herds to store and fat cattle, except in the neighbourhood of Birmingham and Coventry. Both cities were ringed by a belt of small dairy farms, often with herds of only between ten and thirty cows, which supplied milk to the growing towns. Cheese-making declined substantially as the century progressed, and farmers looked increasingly to meat production, again for the urban market including, in this instance, London. Robert Bakewell had also experimented with cattle breeding, but less successfully. More important and effectual was the work of 'Mr Webster of Canley, near Coventry, and Mr Fowler, of Rollewright', though they, like Bakewell, were working with longhorn breeds, and the greatest advances were to come in the 19th century with shorthorns. Most farms had a few pigs, as did many cottages, while poultry, too, were ubiquitous. However, on the Earl of Craven's estate at Coombe Abbey, turkeys were being commercially raised in the early 19th century for the London and Birmingham markets. The increasing importance of the Birmingham market for food is also reflected in the area of potato

100 *Reaping wheat at Tredington, 1901. The men are reaping with sickles and the women, clad in canvas aprons, tie the sheaves. In the foreground is the midday meal basket with 'boiled bacon, new potatoes, currant roly poly pudding and a large can of tea'*

and vegetable small-holdings around the city and along the Tame valley towards Coleshill in the early 19th century, and the growing significance from the late 19th century onwards of orchards and early vegetable farms in the parishes of Salford Priors and Bidford-on-Avon, the natural extension of the Vale of Evesham.

The 19th Century

Great houses continued to be built in the 19th century, many of them supported by industrial rather than agricultural wealth. The finest house is probably Ettington Park, built in 1858-62 for the Shirley family, lords of the manor from early medieval times. It is in early Gothic style and has much fine sculpture representing events in the history of the Shirley family. There are Victorian 'castles' at Studley, built in 1833 for Sir Francis Goodricke, and at Merevale, home of the Dugdales, which was built in 1840 and still contains the library assembled in the 17th century by Sir William Dugdale, the Warwickshire antiquary. Around Birmingham, Aston Hall was occupied by James Watt in the early 19th century; Highbury Hall was built for Joseph Chamberlain in 1879-80, and a number of houses were built for, or occupied by, the Cadbury family.

To operate these great houses a whole army of servants was needed, and through the 19th century the majority of young women living in the countryside and country towns spent a period between leaving school and marriage 'in service'. At Charlecote, a relatively small house, in 1851 no less than 15 servants lived in the house, including a housekeeper, cook, six maids, butler, valet, footman, and page, while there were a coachman and groom to look after the horses, and three or four gardeners and carpenters who lived in the village at Charlecote. Almost as well-provided for was John Lucy, rector of nearby Hampton Lucy, a living normally reserved for a younger son of the Lucys of Charlecote. John was a 60-year-old bachelor in 1851, but he had a housekeeper and four female and three male servants ministering to his needs and running his house and garden for him. There would have been rather fewer servants in the 17th- and 18th-century country houses. In the countryside rates of pay were much lower than in towns and agricultural labourers earned only between twelve and fourteen shillings a week. Stockmen and waggoners could earn a couple of shillings more, but their hours of work were longer, and similarly carpenters and builders, whose wages compared with the town-dweller.

During the agricultural boom of the early 1870s, Joseph Arch, a hedge-cutter and Primitive Methodist preacher from Barford, began to organise agricultural labourers into a union demanding better wages. In 1872 labourers in the Wellesbourne area went on strike and, after a meeting in Leamington, the Warwickshire Agricultural Labourers' Union was formed. Local and national publicity ensured the success of the strikers within a few weeks and a month later, with the help of Liberal politicians from Birmingham, Arch formed a national union. The great agricultural depression after 1875

101 *Cottage at Aston Cantlow, 1892. Rural cottages often had only two or three small rooms with sleeping accommodation high in the rafters. Water was brought from a village pump in pails and cottagers had few possessions*

unfortunately undid many of the improvements and wages fell back to earlier levels.

Two other sets of buildings were greatly affected by the attentions of the landed aristocracy and the gentry—villages and parish churches. Both were rebuilt to accord with the architectural and landscape fashions of the age, churches often in concert with the rebuilding of the mansion, but villages normally in the 19th century, as the spirit of paternalism and philanthropy grew stronger. The new estate villages were usually 'closed', that is to say they were entirely owned by the great landowner who could determine who lived there. Most inhabitants would work on the estate. Perhaps the best group of estate villages are those on the Alscot estate in the Stour valley. Here the Roberts-West family improved rural housing in Alderminster,

Wimpstone, and Preston-upon-Stour in the mid-19th century. The cottages are attractive red brick 'Gothic' houses in semi-detached pairs with large gardens. At Preston the church was also rebuilt, and a school provided. Combrook is another attractive estate village, this time in Elizabethan style, and built to replace the village cleared away when the great park at Compton Verney was created. Walton, too, is in Tudor style, built in 1867 to the design of Giles Gilbert Scott, at the same time as the hall built for Sir Charles Mordaunt. To modern eyes life in such closed estate villages might seem impossibly restricted, but cottages were usually kept in good repair, living conditions were far better than in the burgeoning towns and the hovels of the 'open' villages and, providing one served the estate well, old age was often made secure from the horrors of the Union workhouse; several pauper widows lived in estate cottages in Charlecote in the mid-19th century, for example.

Churches were altered both inside and out. From the later medieval period onwards they were repositories for the spectacular funeral monuments of great landowners, so that in churches such as Compton Wynyates the whole building is filled with memorials of stone or glass. The style of the monuments changed, of course, from kneeling Tudor effigies such as those to Robert Price and his wife at Churchover of 1595; through classical busts, such as the early pair at Chesterton to Sir Edward and Lady Peyto by John Stone; to Baroque figures such as that to Sir William Boughton at Newbold-on-Avon made in 1716. In other villages the whole church was rebuilt in the 18th century to fit into the classical landscape. At Compton Verney, 'Capability' Brown himself designed the new church in 1772, a plain Georgian building. More spectacular, and perhaps the finest church of the late 18th century in England was the new church at Great Packington, built in 1789-90 to the designs of the Italian architect, Bonomi. Its classical brick square with corner towers is an important part of the park landscape. Church rebuilding continued into the 19th century, including the fine church at Hampton Lucy, rebuilt to the designs of Thomas Rickman, with a prominent tower which was an important 'eye-catcher' from the windows of Charlecote. But these country churches are outnumbered by the many new churches provided in the growing towns and cities.

8

The Development of Industry: 1660-1900

Road Transport

Warwickshire's location on the 'watershed of England' meant that it contained only one navigable river within its boundaries, the Avon, and that was navigable only as far as Stratford. Road transport was therefore of vital significance to the well-being of trade and industry in the county. Road maintenance was the responsibility of the manorial lord in the medieval period, though some bridges and causeways were maintained by religious guilds founded for this purpose. The bridge over the Avon at Stratford is a still-standing example of this manorial responsibility since it was provided by Sir Hugh Clopton in the late 15th century. The 'sumptuous new bridge of stone, where in the middle be 6 great arches for the main streame of Avon' replaced a 'poore bridge of tymber and no causey [causeway] to come to it', whose state meant that many people 'refusyd to cum to Stratford when the Avon was up, or coming thither stoode in jeopardy of lyfe'. By the 16th century this system had broken down and so in 1555 an Act was passed 'for amending of Highways being both very noisom and tedious to travel in, and dangerous to all passengers and carriages'. This Act transferred the obligation to repair roads to the parishes. Each year a surveyor of highways was chosen in every parish who called out all able-bodied men to work on the roads for four, and subsequently for six, days while those who possessed carts had to bring them along.

From the mid-17th century surveyors were able to levy rates of up to sixpence in the pound to purchase materials for repair, while the fines imposed by county justices on those summoned for not carrying out their statute labour were also put to the costs of repair. In parishes without very heavy soils and without main routes running through them this worked well and all roads received a fair share of maintenance. However, where clay soil led to rapid deterioration of tracks after heavy rain, or where heavily-used routes traversed a parish, there was manifest unfairness and it is not surprising that parishioners objected to repairing roads used principally by others. As the number of carts, pack-horses, coaches, and riders using the main routes increased steadily through the 17th century, by the end of the century many of these roads were in appalling condition and were often impassable for long periods in the winter. Even in summer road travel could be very slow.

Celia Fiennes, in 1697, set out from Warwick to cover the 14 miles to Daventry 'all along part of the Vale of the Red Horse which was very heavy way and could not reach thither'. Night fell as they reached Shuckburgh, only 11 miles on from Warwick, and Sir Charles Shuckburgh took pity on the travellers and their 'horses weary with the heavy way'.

In 1662, a new means of financing main road improvement was devised— the turnpike. On a turnpike, gates were set up at either end of the road and tolls were collected from the users; this money was then applied to maintaining the road. At first the county justices administered this system, but in 1707 two Acts passed through Parliament which set up trustees to run turnpikes. One of these was for the road from Old Stratford, in Northamptonshire, to Dunchurch, near Rugby. Warwickshire thereby obtained its first four miles of turnpike road. Roads were turnpiked on local initiative, not by government decree. However, national and local initiative often coincided. The earliest stretches of road improved in Warwickshire were those running south-east to north-west across the county which were part of the national road network linking London, Birmingham, Shrewsbury, Chester, Liverpool, and Holyhead. All these roads had to cross the Midland clay vales and, as Daniel Defoe had perceived in his travels, on the road 'to Coventry and from thence to Chester the deep clays reach through all the towns of ... Dunchurch, Coventry, Coleshill and even to Birmingham for very nearly 80 miles'. The road from Dunchurch to Meriden, through Coventry, was turnpiked in 1723, the alternative roads from Banbury to Birmingham, through Warwick and through Stratford-upon-Avon, both in 1725; and that from Oxford, through Shipston-on-Stour, to Stratford in 1729. From Birmingham, both the Bristol and Holyhead roads were turnpiked in 1726. Turnpiking did not necessarily mean substantial improvement in the early 18th century. Much of the toll income was swallowed up in paying the wages of gatekeepers, surveyors and labourers and servicing the debt incurred in

102 *Warwickshire turnpike roads*

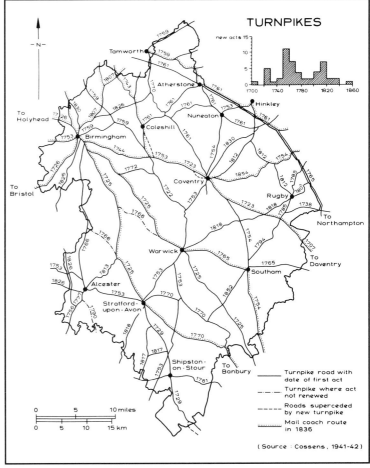

(Source : Cossens, 1941-42)

103 *Tollhouse on the Alcester-Stratford Turnpike. This road was turnpiked in 1753 but the toll-house dates from the early 19th century. Originally the road was gated and all traffic using it had to pay a toll for the upkeep of the carriageway*

building the tollhouses. Many travellers sought to avoid the tolls by taking alternative routes and, in the Feldon, it remained difficult to obtain suitable stone and gravel to effect repairs. However, conditions were marginally better and mail coaches began to ply from London to Holyhead, Liverpool and Shrewsbury through Warwickshire. Tolls on the Birmingham to Edge Hill turnpike through Stratford varied from 3d. to 1s. for coaches, depending on the number of horses and from 2d. to 8d. for carts. Farm animals were charged by the score, sheep at 5d., cattle at 10d.

Between 1750 and 1770 a large number of new Turnpike Acts added very substantially to the mileage of turnpike roads, especially in the north-east of the county. The Liverpool mail route along Watling Street, with alternative diversions through Hinckley and Nuneaton, was turnpiked in 1761. The final phase of turnpike formation came between 1800 and 1820 and this improved many of the 'cross routes', such as the roads between Warwick and Rugby, and Birmingham and Sutton Coldfield. Most of these turnpikes improved existing roads; there were few completely new stretches, but they included part of the old Holyhead mail route around the Earl of Aylesford's park at Packington, part of the Banbury road around Castle Park at Warwick, the Pershore road out of Birmingham, and part of Telford's Holyhead road on either side of Coventry.

The coaching industry

As the network of turnpikes became more comprehensive and the trusts better administered, journey times were dramatically reduced. By the mid-18th century it was possible to reach London from Birmingham in 36 hours in summer, and by the end of the century a traveller could be reasonably certain of making the journey in 15 hours, even in winter, whereas in 1700

104 *The London-Birmingham stage-coach, 1731*

it normally took three or four days. By 1837, the Holyhead Mail was scheduled to do the 110 miles to Birmingham in 11 hours 8 minutes. These reductions in journey time and increasing reliability of services were accomplished in a number of ways: stage-coaches were made less solidly and built of lighter materials since they were no longer subject to heavily-rutted roads; the better roads meant that they could travel faster and more safely and could also continue after dark; competing stage-coach companies were continually trying to improve journey times by changing horses at frequent intervals, and methods of road repair were becoming more scientifically based. Such travel was certainly not cheap, and fares rose quite steeply through the 18th century from an average of just over 2d. a mile in 1750 to 4½d. per mile in 1808.

105   *Carrier's cart*

Between 1770 and 1835 coaching was a major industry and source of employment, especially in the country towns through which main routes passed. Places such as Atherstone, Coleshill, Henley-in-Arden, Shipston-on-Stour, and Southam began to flourish again, while even in established towns such as Rugby, Warwick and Stratford coaching played a major part in the economy. Horses had to be stabled and shod, harness needed constant maintenance, coaches needed repair and, most of all, passengers needed to be fed and accommodated on overnight stops. The inns from which coach services departed were therefore often rebuilt at the end of the 18th century to provide large numbers of bedrooms, big public rooms, stabling and repair sheds, and a through access from front to back so that coaches did not have to turn round in crowded inn yards. Such inns included the *Castle* hotel and *George* inn in Warwick, the *Swan* and the *Hen and Chickens* in Birmingham; and the *Red Horse* and the *Shakespeare* in Stratford. In the 1830s several dozen coaches a day were passing through Birmingham and Coventry, while there were 12 even in Stratford.

106   *The London to Birmingham mail coach. Journey times between the capital and Birmingham were reduced to a little over eleven hours by the 1830s. In the mid-18th century it took 36 hours or more*

107 *A Birmingham coaching inn. Coach services ran from large courtyard inns in towns and cities such as the* St George's Tavern *in Birmingham High Street. Such inns were a major source of employment*

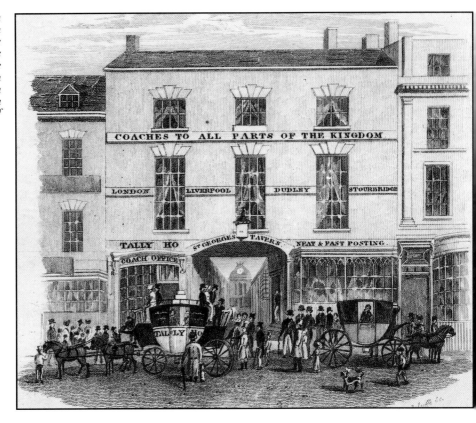

Passenger transport was not alone in benefiting from the improved state of the roads; goods carriage was similarly affected. In the early 18th century heavy wagons were used for some goods, but most smaller items went by pack-horse. Heavy or bulky items were extremely expensive to transport by road. By the mid-18th century a network of carriers had come into being, taking goods between the principal towns in broad-wheeled wagons and, by the end of the century, this network had been extended to the smaller towns and large villages. The country carriers often lived in the village rather than town, and combined their carrying with another occupation, such as inn-keeper, carpenter, or small-holder. On the market days of nearby towns they would set out early in the morning collecting packages, and often passengers, from all the villages en route to the market. In the late afternoon they would make the return journey, often a little the worse for drink, since the carrier network, too, was focused on the urban inn. Stage-coaches could not meet the competition of the railways, and by the mid-1840s most of the main companies had succumbed. Carriers were more flexible, however, and though the long-distance routes were given up to the railways, carriers continued to provide goods transport to the villages until the advent of the motor bus in the early 20th century. In Southam, as late as 1884 there were three carriers. Andrew Hough and William Tyler went to Banbury on Thursdays, and

Coventry on Tuesdays and Fridays, while Simon Warner travelled to Daventry on Wednesdays, and Leamington on Mondays, Thursdays and Saturdays, the latter journey being extended to Warwick. All three men lived in the town.

The Canals

Despite the comprehensive network of turnpikes and the increased efficiency of both passenger and goods transport, there remained no satisfactory means of transporting heavy or bulky goods in the mid-18th century. Only in the south-west did the Avon Navigation, formed in 1639, allow 'a very great trade for sugar, oil, wine, tobacco, iron, lead and in a word all heavy goods ... and in return the corn, and especially the cheese is brought back from Gloucestershire and Warwick here to Bristol'. The greatest need of the developing industrial economy of the 18th century was for a method of transporting coal cheaply and efficiently. The invention of the canal met that need. The West Midland canals had two objects: first they provided cheap transport for heavy bulk goods such as coal, iron, limestone, clay and manufactured goods, and second, they were planned to connect the manufacturing districts with deep-water ports and the wider national and international markets for their produce. The earliest canal to be initiated was the Birmingham canal in 1768, designed to bring Black Country coal and iron into the manufacturing and commercial heart of the region. The second series of canals ringed the north and eastern sides of the county and eventually linked Birmingham to London. The Coventry canal linked Tamworth to Coventry via Nuneaton, effectively integrating the manufacturing districts of the east Warwickshire coalfield, while the Oxford canal linked Coventry and Rugby and then meandered through the south Warwickshire countryside to cross the Jurassic scarp near Banbury. Both these canals were completed during the 'Canal Mania' of the 1770s. The final link was provided by the Birmingham and Fazeley Canal opened in 1789. The shorter 'Grand Union' route through Warwick was completed in 1800, while other canals were built during the Napoleonic Wars to link Birmingham to Worcester, and to Stratford-upon-Avon.

108 *Lift bridge, Stratford Canal*

By 1815, Birmingham was at the hub of a national network of canals, the centre of a cross linking the four estuaries of Thames, Severn, Mersey, and Humber, and this was despite its unpromising plateau-top site. In order to reach Birmingham canals had to ascend this plateau and there are thus long flights of locks on each—at Hatton on the Warwick and Birmingham, at Tardebigge on the Birmingham and Worcester, and the Farmer's Bridge flight on the Birmingham and Fazeley. In order to keep locks to a minimum the early canals contoured around hillsides. This is particularly noticeable on the Oxford canal around Wormleighton since Earl Spencer only permitted the canal to be built over his land if there were no locks and wharves to encourage boatmen to stop there. In the 19th century the techniques of making cuttings and embankments were improved, and some of these loops were shortened, for example, near Brinklow. In Birmingham such was the

109 *Canal narrow boat c.1910. Canal boat operators often lived with their families in cramped cabins on the horse-drawn narrow boats. Coal made up the great majority of cargoes but general merchandise was also carried*

density of boats and the chaos of horses on the towpath that a completely new Birmingham canal was cut in the 1820s, engineered by Thomas Telford. It ran broad and straight from Birmingham to Smethwick, with a towpath on each bank and with the loops of the older canal linked to it, as they were by then lined with factories. To supply the summit levels of the canals there were large reservoirs at Rotten Park in Birmingham, at Earlswood, and at several points along the Jurassic scarp.

The opening of a canal was always attended by joyous celebrations in towns through which it passed. These were partly a good advertisement for companies using the canal, but mostly were a genuine expression of pleasure, since almost invariably the price of coal fell substantially once the canal was available to transport it. New industries often followed directly, especially to the major wharfs at Warwick, Stratford, Rugby, and Nuneaton. Canal carriers operated in much the same way as their road counterparts with regular services of 'fly boats'. These averaged 3-3½ m.p.h., carried 10 tons of goods, a crew of four, worked for 24 hours a day and had priority over other boats at locks. Horses were changed every ten or twelve miles in order to keep up speed since competition between carriers was fierce. On most canals in the early 19th century there were between five and ten boats operating daily in each direction, and many of the services linked well beyond Warwickshire. Besides this general merchandise, however, huge quantities of coal were being transported, and for most years well over 50 per cent of goods carried consisted of coal. Limestone, lime, especially on the Warwick and Napton, manure, and road materials were also important. It is mostly forgotten today that there were passenger boats on many canals, too. Tonnage rates

110 *Lock-keeper's cottage, Lowsonford*

were usually specified in the Acts of Parliament, and varied from 1½d. to 4d. per ton per mile, with higher charges for shorter distances, especially where these involved passing through locks.

The East Warwickshire Coalfield

The Warwickshire coalfield is one of several small Midland coalfields. The coal measures are exposed in a narrow outcrop running from just south of Tamworth to Coventry and they dip steeply downwards to the west. At a depth of about 1,000 feet the coal seams level out, and, in fact, underlie much of north-east Warwickshire. However, this 'concealed' coalfield was completely unknown to the coalmasters and miners until the mid-19th century and until then mining activities were intensively concentrated in the narrow, exposed part of the coalfield, especially between Coventry and Nuneaton.

The market potential of Coventry for sales, especially from the early 17th century when the uses of coal began to multiply, was reflected in an outburst of mining activity at this time. There were mines at Dordon, in the north, and at Nuneaton, Griff, Bedworth, Foleshill, Sowe, and Wyken, the last three known collectively as Coventry colliery, since they were leased out by Coventry Corporation. The major problem encountered in working the coal was drainage and as the mines went deeper more and more money had to be invested in drainage works. There were baling engines or 'gins' worked by horses, adit-like tunnels called soughs to take the water away, and water pits. There was little difficulty with gas, though there was an occasional fire: payments were made at Griff in the early 17th century for 'filling the top of the pit where the fire bred' and 'stopping the Eare pitt with earth to damp the fire out'.

Some of the most notable mining entrepreneurs of the day were attracted to the Coventry part of the coalfield, including Huntingdon Beaumont, in 1595, and subsequently his brother, Sir Thomas Beaumont. Sir Thomas took a 31-year lease on the Coventry mines for £40 per annum rising to £200 when 'he shall finde sufficient delphe'. However, he surrendered his lease early as the costs of drainage proved too much and the Coventry mines closed in 1688 for an extended period. A little further north, near Bedworth, another mine proved much less troublesome, and for a short time coal was pouring into Coventry, reducing the price from 11d. to 8d. per hundredweight. The miners worked with pick and shovel filling wicker baskets with the coal and were paid by the 'three quarters', normally 10d. per three quarters, while ale was given to those 'deservinge it by following their woorke'.

The two most important mines in the 17th century were those at Bedworth and Griff and during the 1630s an output of between 20,000 and 30,000 tons is recorded at Bedworth. However, such an output was sporadic and on average most mines operated only one year in three at this period. Bedworth had been abandoned in 1618 by Sir Thomas Beaumont because of flooding, causing great distress in the village since its inhabitants were entirely dependent upon the mine for employment. It was re-opened by a three-man partnership,

111 *Water-operated bucket chain*

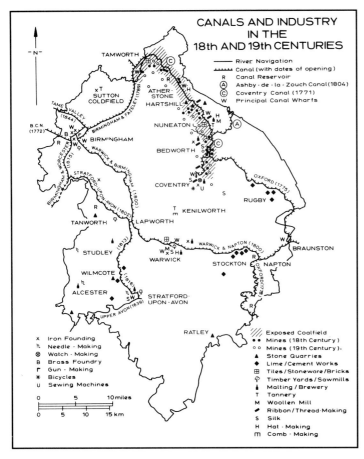

CANALS AND INDUSTRY IN THE 18th AND 19th CENTURIES

River Navigation
Canal (with dates of opening)
R Canal Reservoir
(A) Ashby-de-la-Zouch Canal (1804)
(C) Coventry Canal (1771)
W Principal Canal Wharfs

x Iron Founding
ꜧ Needle-Making
⊗ Watch-Making
B Brass Foundry
ꞃ Gun-Making
✳ Bicycles
U Sewing Machines

0   5   10 miles
0   5   10   15 km

/// Exposed Coalfield
• • Mines (18th Century)
o o Mines (19th Century)
▲ Stone Quarries
◆ Lime/Cement Works
⊞ Tiles/Stoneware/Bricks
φ Timber Yards/Sawmills
⌁ Malting/Brewery
T Tannery
M Woollen Mill
◢ Ribbon/Thread-Making
S Silk
H Hat-Making
m Comb-Making

112 *Canals and industries in the 18th and 19th centuries*

113 *Whim Gin*

who for a few years had a practical monopoly of the local trade. A group of Coventry men re-opened Griff colliery in 1622 to break this monopoly and there then ensued an unsavoury running battle, over a period of three decades, between the two mines. Court records show accusations of deliberately flooded workings and the turning of polluted water across the competitors' meadows so that some horses died.

Between 1700 and 1710, Sir Richard Newdigate II, of Arbury Hall, on whose land Griff was situated, tried to create a large and heavily capitalised colliery. Special attention was paid to the drainage arrangements along the whole two miles of the outcrop with soughs, horse-powered gins and wind and water pumps. His initial investment was well over £4,000 and in some years large quantities of coal were raised, over 16,000 tons in 1705, but he failed to make his fortune. The early 18th century is noteworthy for the introduction of steam engines to solve the problems of draining the mines. Thomas Newcomen had intended to erect his first commercial engine at Griff in 1711, but in the event Griff had to wait until 1714, and the first engine went to Dudley, in Staffordshire. Though they efficiently drained the mines the economics of operating these early engines was not easy. They were expensive to operate, there were patent fees to pay, and they devoured vast quantities of coal—so much so that it was quite possible for an engine to consume all the coal raised, with none left to sell. There was continued mismanagement, litigation and even occasional sabotage. As a result many of the larger collieries closed in the mid-18th century: Griff in 1730 for 40 years; Hawkesbury in 1732; and Wyken in 1744; but there were many other smaller collieries working the coalfield further north. Henry Beighton's map of 1725 shows over fifty collieries, including a group of seven in the neighbourhood of Wilnecote.

The period between 1770 and 1850 saw a more stable pattern of production in the Warwickshire coalfield, but in the mid-19th century it was the smallest British coalfield with an output of only 255,000 tons in total. The three main collieries remained those at Griff, Hawkesbury and Wyken, the first two having re-opened in the 1770s and Wyken in the 1790s. Their development was closely linked with the construction of the Coventry canal which widened the market for their coal. Sir Roger Newdigate of Griff, and Richard Parrott of Hawkesbury, were prime movers in establishing and investing in the canal company, and all three collieries had canal arms coming right to the pithead. There was heavy investment as well in new steam engines and, in 1776, the Hawkesbury colliery purchased from Boulton and Watt what was 'justly supposed to be the most powerful engine in England' for some £4,500.

It was not until 1851 that D.S. Dugdale sank the first deep shafts into the concealed coalfield at Baddesley. Coal was found at a depth of 1,000ft. and the colliery developed rapidly since it was linked by mineral railway to the London & North-Western Railway. Its coal thereby found a ready market in London and by 1865 more than a quarter of its total output was railed to the capital. The discovery of the concealed coalfield and the development of the rail network—all mines were linked by 1880—meant that output from the coalfield as a whole was increasing by 10 per cent per year in the 1850s and 1860s. It reached a peak in 1913 with some five million tons. New deep mines were sunk at Haunchwood, Griff, Kingsbury and Newdigate in the 1890s, and at Arley, Binley and Coventry in the first decade of the 20th century.

114 *Mine shaft head gear, c.1800*

Textile Industries

Cloth manufacture declined in the 16th and 17th centuries and other related trades rose to prominence. Of these, the most important was the making of caps and hats. Caps were knitted from high quality wool and there were several Tudor Acts of Parliament which tried to protect the industry by regulating price and quality, and by making it an offence to wear or sell foreign-made caps or hats. The process of felting, to make hats, was introduced from Spain via the Netherlands in the time of Elizabeth I. The cappers were one of Coventry's richest and most important guilds in the 16th and 17th centuries, but caps were also made in other towns with a cloth industry, including Alcester, Stratford, and Warwick, where the industry was re-established in the 1830s on a factory basis. From the 17th century onwards, however, the main focus of the hat industry moved to north-east Warwickshire where there were hatters in Rugby and Nuneaton and, most particularly, in Atherstone. In the 18th and 19th centuries straw, silk, beaver and felt hats were all made in the town, the small factories being built on the long plots behind the street frontages.

The second textile trade that developed in Coventry was ribbon-making, in this instance, at the beginning of the 18th century. Defoe comments upon the significance of the black ribbon trade in the 1720s and the industry continued to be important until the 1870s. Ribbon-making was probably introduced by emigré French workers and there was continuing competition with French products in terms of both colours and qualities, while the vagaries of fashion in clothing regulated the prosperity of the ribbon-weavers. In 1815 nearly half of Coventry's population, some 10,000 men and women, were engaged in ribbon-making and the industry was also important at

115 *Early 19th-century mine engine*

116 *Ribbon-makers'*
cottages, Coventry

Bedworth, Nuneaton, Atherstone, and the villages around such as Foleshill, Exhall, and Bulkinton. The scale of production increased in the 1850s and steam-powered machinery was introduced, not without violent protest, as the burning in 1831 of Beck's factory in Coventry shows. The 1830s were times of great distress for the cottage ribbon-weavers, partly because of the introduction of factory methods, and partly because of the competition of cheaper French and Swiss products. However, the industry recovered and in the late 1850s there were some 25,000 people employed in and around Coventry in 15 large factories and some 300 'cottage' factories, the latter having from two to six looms. During the 1860s the cottage weavers began to decline rapidly in the face of foreign competition and, after a brief period of prosperity in the early 1870s, the final decline set in. The cottage factories of Coventry's ribbon-makers formed a very distinctive part of the townscape until recently. Terraced cottages were built with the top floor adapted to house the loom. These 'top shops' had continuous windows to throw maximum light on the machinery, and the cottagers would subscribe to a steam engine to supply the whole row of cottages, the engine shaft running along under the roof.

A high proportion of the ribbons were made of silk, and silk cloth was also manufactured in the area. There was a mill in Coventry, and a large manufactory was established in Nuneaton in 1891. Cotton cloth had enjoyed a period of prosperity in the early 19th century, notably at Fazeley, Sir Robert Peel's mills just over the Warwickshire border near Tamworth; but there were also mills in Coventry and Nuneaton. The same period saw a steam-powered woollen mill established at Warwick beside the canal basin where coal could be bought in cheaply. Thread-making was a Coventry trade of medieval origin when the deep blue dyes were especially highly regarded, and it continued on a small scale into the 19th century in both Birmingham and Coventry. Gloves, too, were made in medieval Coventry, but this industry was more especially connected with Stratford in the 16th and 17th centuries when there were at least seven glovers in the town.

Quarrying

The variety of rocks underlying Warwickshire has been extensively exploited through the centuries for different purposes. William Stukeley noticed the 'good stone dug up at hand' at Warwick, while the making of Coventry Cross, in 1541-4, was to be of 'good, sound and reasonable stone from the quarries of Attleborough and Rowington'. Rowington stone was also used in the construction of St Philip's, Birmingham, in the early 18th century. The Lower Lias limestone was extensively quarried in the south and east, near Stockton, Harbury, Wilmcote, Binton, Grafton, and Rugby, which was the most substantial of the 19th-century quarries. Wilmcote stone was used for paving the Houses of Parliament and Royal Courts of Justice. Cement-making is a major industry of the 19th and 20th centuries in the vicinity of Rugby and Stockton. The Lias limestone and clay form the raw materials,

while first the canal, and, subsequently, the railways enabled this heavy and bulky product to be trans-shipped. The lime works in Warwickshire are similarly closely tied to the canals. The marls near Nuneaton provided the raw materials for two factories making tiles, earthenware and terra-cotta, but pottery-making was not especially important in the county.

117 *Brickworks and colliery near Nuneaton, 1950. Local clays were extracted for brick and tile making from Roman times around Nuneaton. The conical tip heap marks the site of Griff No.4 Colliery*

Metal Manufacturing

Of overwhelming importance is the myriad variety of metal-manufacturing trades upon which Birmingham built its fame and fortune, and which were also of some significance in other areas of the county. Leland's description of Birmingham in 1540 where 'there be many smithes in the towne that use to make knives and all maner of cuttynge tools, and many lorimars that make byts, and a great many naylors. So that a great part of the towne is mayntayned by smithes' is well-known and shows the variety of iron trades already established in the 16th century. Although iron manufacturing was important, and was to become more so in the 17th century, the real prosperity of Birmingham was based upon its ironmongers, who were the equivalent of Coventry's cloth merchants, middlemen getting bar iron from the forge and passing it to the smith, then selling the smiths' products to customers over an ever-widening market area. Among the more important families involved were the Colemores, the Smalbrokes and the Kinges, who were all to play a part in Birmingham's later development. Of the 16th-century manufactures, probably the most important was the making of cutlery, edge

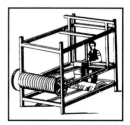

118 *Wireworker*

tools and swords, and this continued into the 19th century, when cutlery declined in favour of the growing Sheffield industry. Many of Birmingham's swords were exported and there was a flourishing market with the U.S.A. in the early 19th century.

Nail-making was widespread in the north-west of Warwickshire, as well as the neighbouring areas of Worcestershire and Staffordshire, and in the rural areas it was a cottage industry in which a reasonable living could be made. During the 18th century the industry began to concentrate in north Worcestershire and south Staffordshire, and Birmingham nailers tended to be merchants rather than manufacturers. It became increasingly difficult to get a good price for hand-made nails as Birmingham merchants invested in machinery, and, during the early 19th century, nailers worked long hours for little return in their cottage nail-shops. The first steam-powered nail factory was built in Birmingham in 1811—the Brittania works—and cottage nailers gradually declined. Screws were another Birmingham industry, and they were at first hand-made by a laborious process. Again, steam-powered machinery was invented in the early 19th century for their manufacture, and by 1850 more than 1,500 people were employed. The largest of the late 19th-century firms was that of Messrs. Nettlefold and Chamberlain.

Perhaps the most important of the 18th-century metal trades in Birmingham was the 'toy-trade', divided between its heavy iron and steel 'toys' such as the tools and implements of carpenters, coopers, gardeners, masons, plumbers, shoemakers, and the like (which included well over 200 different kinds of hammer!) and the light toy trade. Light toys included the manufacture of buckles, brooches, watch chains, key rings and candle-snuffers. The manufacture of each toy was often further divided into firms specialising in stamping, burnishing or plating, while products were constantly changing so that as one item went out of fashion another would be introduced. The variety of goods, and of the firms making them, was of the highest order. There was a similar organisation into smaller firms in the jewellery industry which

119 *Britannia plated 'toys'*

was of growing significance in 18th-century Birmingham, and in the gun and button industries. Buttons were made in Coventry and Stratford in the 16th century, but by the 18th century it had become another of Birmingham's 1,001 trades. Other iron trades included casting and the making of machinery, wire drawing, and die stamping, which included the making of coins.

One metal industry not concentrated in Birmingham was the manufacture of needles, which though now associated with the Worcestershire town of Redditch was, in the 18th century, centred in the parish of Studley. The wire from which they were made came from Birmingham and the wholesale merchants also lived there, but the Arrow valley between Studley and Alcester was the manufacturing area. Machinery and steam power improved production from the late 1820s. Pins, thimbles and hooks and eyes were made in Birmingham. The making of combs from horn and from ivory was a small but growing industry centred in Kenilworth in the early 19th century. There were nine comb-makers in 1835, 12 in 1850, but none in 1884. Brewing had moved from a home-based to a factory industry in the 19th century, but

remained sufficiently localised for almost every town to have its own brewery. The larger breweries were close to the canals through which they obtained their raw materials. Other metals than iron were worked, of which the most significant was probably brass, again centred in Birmingham. The first brass foundry was established in 1740 and within forty years the various branches of the trade were consuming 1,000 tons per annum. The objects were closely related to the small iron objects on which the city had made its fortune, and included weights and measures, ornaments, cabinet handles, hinges, candlesticks, plumbers' materials, and, in the mid-19th century, brass bedsteads. Bedsteads were exported all over the world and, in the 1860s, were being made at the rate of 5,000 a week. By the mid-1880s this had quadrupled, and some forty firms were involved. Bell-founding is an allied trade, but it is not well represented in Warwickshire. There were bellfounders in Stratford in the 17th century, and in Birmingham in the 18th and 19th centuries, but none of first rank. There were glass-makers of first rank, however, in both medieval and modern times. Coventry glaziers were well known in the 14th and 15th centuries and, in 1405, John Thornton was commissioned to glaze the great east window of York Minster. He was one of the most notable glass-painters of the age and the contract stipulated that he had to execute

120 *Cartland's Brass foundry, 1897, one of Birmingham's many brassworks specialising in brass fittings for builders and for furniture. Some 700 people were employed in this works and the casting shop, shown here, was one of the most advanced in Britain*

121 *Interior of bedstead makers, 1902. Brass bedsteads from Birmingham were exported all over the world in the second half of the 19th century. Fisher, Brown & Bayley of Lionel Street were one of some forty firms involved in manufacture*

the whole work himself. In Birmingham, glass-making seems to have developed from the button trade when there was a demand for glass buttons in the mid-18th century. By the 1820s there were at least ten glass firms in Birmingham making everything from glass buttons to the finest cut glass objects, but the largest firm was that of Messrs. Chance at Spon Lane, Smethwick, founded in 1815, who made crown and sheet glass.

Watches and Bicycles

There remain three Coventry-based industries to consider. Clocks and watches came into domestic use in the early 17th century, and by the 1660s the making of watches was already established in Coventry. As with the Birmingham toy and jewellery trades, it was an industry which lent itself to extreme division of labour and by the early 19th century over 100 branches of the trade could be listed. The most important was the finisher, since it was he who put the pieces together and set the watch in motion. By the 1850s there were some 2,000 watchmakers in Coventry employing over 3,000 apprentices, so that it was second only to the ribbon industry. There were watchmakers in other towns, notably in Birmingham, where there were perhaps 600 to 700, many of them women, but here they were essentially repairers rather than makers.

Because of the skills of the watchmakers the Coventry Sewing Machine Company was established in 1863 to use some of those skills, but lack of capital and fierce American competition meant that, though the company survived, it did not flourish. In 1868, they were persuaded to diversify and take an order from France for 400 'bone-shaker' bicycles. The Franco-Prussian war prevented delivery and the firm looked to develop a home market. So began the industry that was to carry Coventry through the last quarter of the 19th century. It was yet another industry in the West Midlands tradition whereby components were made by a myriad of small firms and then assembled into the finished product. The Coventry Machine Company, which became Swift Cycles in 1896, was quickly joined by other small firms, and by 1881 perhaps 400 people were employed in the industry. By 1885 this had grown to some 3,000, and by 1890 to 4,000, while there were over half that number employed in Birmingham and Aston, the next largest centre. This rapid expansion in the 1880s was due to the development, first of the popular penny-farthing, then of the tricycle, and finally of the safety bicycle, the basis of modern cycle design. Tricycles were especially popular for commercial house-to-house deliveries and were adopted by the Post Office for a period. The introduction of the tandem in 1882, Dunlop's pneumatic tyres in 1892, the free-wheel in 1897, and the three-speed gear in 1903, ensured the continued popularity of cycles and, in 1896, the Premier Cycle Company claimed that its Coventry works was the largest in the world with an annual output of over 20,000 machines.

122 Coventry watchmaker, c.1920. Watchmaking was one of Coventry's most important industries in the 19th century. There were over one hundred branches of the trade. Most craftsmen, like this jewel-maker, worked on benches set beneath long windows to provide good light

The Railways

Warwickshire's first railway was not intended to compete with the canals, but to serve them. The Stratford and Moreton Railway Act was passed in 1821 and the 16 miles of line was opened in 1826. It ran from the canal basin at the Bancroft in Stratford, over the Avon and through the south Warwickshire countryside to Moreton-in-Marsh, with a branch to Shipton-on-Stour. The line was engineered by John Rastrick, a West Midlands iron founder, at an estimated cost of £33,500 and Viscount Dudley was one of the principal promoters and share-holders of the company. The railway, which was horse drawn, enabled Black Country coal brought down the Stratford canal to be distributed through south-west Warwickshire and the north Cotswolds, while lime, stone and agricultural products were taken northwards. The county's next two lines were of much greater significance. The Grand Junction Railway, opened in 1837, linked Manchester and Liverpool to Birmingham, and the London and Birmingham Railway was opened the following year.

123 *Rover   safety bicycle, 1885*

124 *Stratford and Moreton Railway, horse-drawn waggon*

The Grand Junction, engineered by Joseph Locke, a young assistant of George Stephenson, passed through Warwickshire only for the first few miles of its route as it circled Birmingham to the north on its way to Wolverhampton. The Acts authorising the two lines received the royal Assent on the same day in 1833 and it was planned that both would be opened together. In the event constructional difficulties delayed the London line. The circuitous route of the Grand Junction out of Birmingham enabled the line to avoid tunnelling under Aston Park, which had been the original intention, but there had been vehement objections from James Watt, the occupier. The line terminated in a temporary station at Vauxhall from where cabs and omnibuses took passengers into the town centre for a shilling. Its opening was viewed by huge and excited crowds despite the fact that the first departure was timed for 7a.m.! The journey to Liverpool of 97 miles took 4½ hours, at an average speed of 22 m.p.h. Thereafter, stage-coaches ran empty and once the London line had opened the major coaching firms operating from Birmingham closed in rapid succession.

125 *Curzon Street station, c.1840. Railway lines to London, Liverpool, Manchester and Gloucester terminated at Curzon Street on the eastern edge of Birmingham. Only later was New Street station in the centre of the city opened*

The line to London, through Hampton-in-Arden, Coventry and Rugby, was severely delayed by engineering problems with the long tunnel at Kilsby in Northamptonshire. The engineers were George and Robert Stephenson and by early 1838 a single track was opened to Rugby with regular trains running between the two towns in April. Hampton-in-Arden was the only other first-class station on this section of the line; Coventry was considered of lesser import! The line terminated at Curzon Street station, on the eastern outskirts of Birmingham, a grand classical portal which still survives, but which was badly adapted for handling passengers. In 1854, the Grand Junction and London and Birmingham having merged to form the London and North Western Railway, the line was extended into the city centre and New Street

station opened. Midland railway traffic began to use it soon after and by the end of the century it had been extended and enlarged to become one of the busiest and biggest stations in Britain.

Lines linking Birmingham to Derby (1839), Gloucester (1840), and Oxford (1852) followed these first two trunk lines. The Oxford line, approved in 1848 and opened in 1852, brought the Great Western Railway's broad gauge tracks into Warwickshire, through Leamington Spa and Solihull, and into a new station in Birmingham at Snow Hill. In the second half of the 19th century further lines were opened through the more rural parts of Warwickshire including, as late as 1908, the 'North Warwickshire' line linking Stratford more directly with Birmingham. The Trent Valley line from Rugby to Stafford was opened to speed rail traffic between London and the north-west by by-passing Birmingham, while also serving Nuneaton, Bedworth and Atherstone. The first sod was cut in November 1845 by the prime minister, Sir Robert Peel, who was M.P. for Tamworth from 1830 to his death in 1850, and the line was especially noted for its iron bridges. Its construction confirmed Rugby as a major railway junction, but though the town expanded as an engineering centre it was never to rival the likes of Crewe or Swindon.

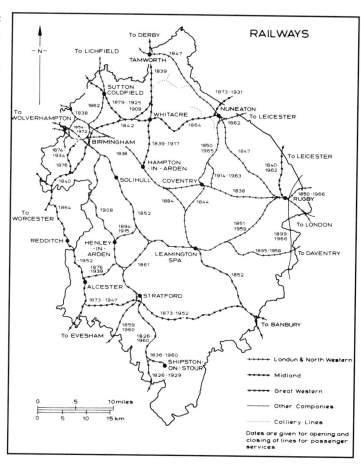

126 *Railways in Warwickshire*

127 *Early locomotive on Grand Junction Railway*

9

The Growing Towns

The pattern of urban growth was by no means fixed and unchanging. Som‹
medieval towns that had sunk into obscurity in the 15th century were neve‹
again to recover their urban status, while other minor medieval marke‹
centres burgeoned into renewed growth in the period between 1700 an‹
1900 as a result of some new functional stimulus. Even as large a city a‹
Coventry was subject to such changes; witness the 16th-century declin‹
there. With the difficulty of assembling population data for the 16th an‹
17th centuries it is not easy to say precisely which towns were growing
Clearly Stratford and Warwick were maintaining their prosperity as th‹
market centres of the Avon valley, despite the effects of fire damage. Clearly
too, Nuneaton and Bedworth were growing quite rapidly through this perio‹

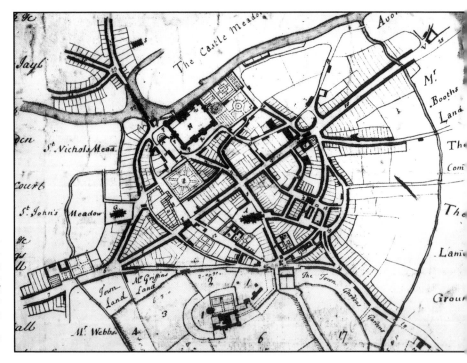

128 *Plan of Warwick, c.1711. Warwick's central cross of streets was destroyed in a fire in 1694. Landscaping of the castle grounds destroyed houses and streets in the late 18th century and a new bridge was built. North is at the bottom of this map*

XI *Landsdowne Crescent, Leamington Spa. Leamington developed in the early 19th century as a spa and residential town. Fortunes were made and lost in the construction of grand Regency terraces such as this and the necessary provision of parks, library, theatres and shops. The visit of Princess Victoria, in 1836, gained the accolade of the 'Royal' prefix.*

XII *The Birmingham and Fazeley Canal. Canals were the arteries of Warwickshire industry from 1760. The national network linked together around Birmingham. In the 1960s and '70s they were atmospheric but derelict. Today they are the focus of townscape renewal schemes as their attractions are increasingly recognised. In the countryside they provide recreation for boating, walkers and fishermen.*

XIII *Inter-war suburban housing, Boldmere. As Birmingham and Coventry grew rapidly in the 1930s, extensive areas of Warwickshire countryside were covered with low-density speculative private housing. Boldmere, to the south of Sutton Park, was attractive because the railway provided easy travel into Birmingham city centre.*

XIV *Centenary Square and the International Convention Centre, Birmingham. The 1990s have seen large areas of Birmingham city centre transformed. The I.C.C. is the centrepiece of a strategy designed to encourage service industry and the arts. The Centre contains one of the world's finest concert halls.*

because of the development of the coalfield, but most other market towns probably stagnated, and, in the 17th century, actually declined. A clear picture emerges with the first national census in 1801. Most of the small towns had a population between one and two thousand, and a century later had rarely more than doubled this. Henley-in-Arden, for example, showed a small decrease, from 1,098 to 1,012 people, as a result of the decline of coaching in the 1830s, but most of the others grew slowly; Southam doubled its population from 900 to 1,800; Coleshill rose from 1,400 to 2,600; and Alcester from 1,600 to 2,300.

129 *Datestone of John Pittway's house, Shipston-on-Stour*

Other towns enjoyed a similar pattern of growth in the 17th and 18th centuries, but then began to grow rapidly in the 19th century. Rugby had only 1,500 inhabitants in 1801, and there was little to distinguish it from other Feldon market centres. However, the rapidly-growing popularity of its public school and the arrival of the London & Birmingham railway meant that by 1851 it was a town of nearly 7,000 people, and by the end of the century continuing industrial development saw the town overspill its bounds into neighbouring Bilton and Hillmorton with a total population of over 21,000. Sutton Coldfield followed a similar, if slightly less spectacular, pattern, though here the mechanism of expansion was the desire of middle-class inhabitants in Birmingham to live in more rural surroundings. The town's population increased from under 3,000 to more than 14,000 through the 19th century. A similar process can be observed beginning in Solihull in the late 19th century. In Nuneaton and Bedworth the development of the East Warwickshire coal-

130 *Rugby School, 1815. Founded in the mid-16th century by Lawrence Sheriffe, it was reconstituted in 1777 and greatly expanded and rebuilt between 1809 and 1820. It became one of the great public schools under Thomas Arnold, headmaster between 1828 and 1842*

131 *Bath Street, Leamington, 1822. The main street of Leamington's first phase of development contained William Abbott's* spa and Bath Hotel *besides three other spas. A theatre opened in 1813 and there was a library and Assembly Rooms by 1822*

132 *Royal Baths and Pump Room, Leamington, 1822*

field and the spin-off of some of Coventry's textile industries meant that these towns were already growing in the 18th century and in 1801 Nuneaton was a town of some 5,000 inhabitants. By the end of the century it had absorbed neighbouring Chilvers Coten and had increased fivefold, while the growth of Bedworth meant that the outcrop of the exposed coalfield was almost continuously built up from Coventry to Hartshill.

The most spectacular pattern of growth, however, took place in a settlement that had been only a small village in 1801 with a population of under five hundred. Leamington Spa expanded dramatically in the 1830s as a fashionable resort, and by mid-century its population had increased thirtyfold. Development continued in the second half of the 19th century as it became a favoured residential abode for those seeking to escape the industrial townscapes of Coventry, and by 1901 it was a town of 23,000 people. Neighbouring Warwick and Kenilworth also developed by attracting this same social group since their castles, historical and literary associations already gave them considerable prestige and tourist potential which was to develop further in the present century. Coventry itself, at the beginning of the 19th century, was already the largest town in the county, excepting Birmingham, with some 16,000 inhabitants and was already overspilling its bounds by absorbing neighbouring villages. By 1851 the flourishing watch and ribbon trades had more than doubled this total, and by the end of the 19th century it was a successful industrial city of over 70,000 people.

Institutions and Government

Such rapid growth inevitably placed considerable strain on both the administration of these towns and upon the ability of landowners, builders and institutions to provide adequate homes and social facilities for the inhabitants. Only Stratford, Sutton Coldfield and Warwick had been incorporated in the 16th century, and even in these towns, together with Coventry, the very limited electorate ensured that administration was bedevilled by oligarchical self-interest. Elsewhere administration was in the hands of the manor court and the parish vestry until the 1840s, and the situation was often little improved until the series of national reforms in the 1870s. Leamington did not obtain borough status until 1875; Nuneaton until 1907; while Rugby had to wait until 1932. There were therefore considerable variations in the ways in which particular towns tackled the problems of water supply, sewage disposal, road maintenance, street lighting, caring for its sick and destitute, and burying the dead. However, in most towns improvements were underway by the 1850s.

133   *Fashionable early 18th-century dress*

Rugby was quite well provided for, partly because there was a high proportion of middle-class residents in the rapidly-growing town, though its rudimentary local government was dominated by the court leet and vestry until a Board of Health was established in 1848. By the mid-19th century the main streets were well paved and were lit by gas supplied by a private company, founded in 1838, which also supplied householders who could afford it. The water supply system was improved in 1852 when a reservoir and pumping station were constructed, and improved again in 1866. A new cemetery was provided in 1863, complete with two mortuary chapels 'and the grounds planted with ornamental shrubs'. Such provision was necessary since the rapid increase in urban populations had completely overwhelmed the capacities of parish churchyards, and in the 1840s many had become a serious danger to health. The reform of the Poor Law in 1832 had made Rugby the centre of a 'Union' of the surrounding parishes and the new workhouse was built on the road towards Hillmorton. The town was also endowed with a remarkable collection of almshouses, out of all proportion to its earlier importance. A hospital was provided only in 1884, through the munificence of R.H. Wood, Esq., who provided some £32,000 to build and endow it. A public park was provided by the Local Board in 1877. This pattern in the provision of public services with its mixture of private benefaction, commercial companies and local government provision is typical of most of the growing 19th-century towns of Warwickshire, though the actual date at which facilities were improved could vary by as much as forty or fifty years. Most towns had gas lighting by the 1840s and the Union workhouse was a nationally imposed reform, but improved water supplies, especially for the poor, often had to wait until the 1860s. At Warwick a new supply was derived from the Avon above the town

134   *Saltisford gas works, Warwick*

in 1857, but this was hardly an improvement, since Kenilworth, Leamington and Coventry were all discharging their sewage into the river further up stream. It was not until a new waterworks was built at Haseley in 1876 that the situation greatly improved, while Warwick's own sewage works followed in 1885. Town halls to house the burgeoning administrative apparatus of the towns were another common addition to the Victorian townscape. That at Leamington was provided in 1884 'in the Renaissance style' and, besides the council chamber and committee rooms, it contained an assembly room exhibition hall, and 'a lofty campanile containing an illuminated clock the gift of Alderman Henry Bright'.

Town Fires

The appearance of most towns changed dramatically between the 17th and 19th centuries. In a few small towns changes were less apparent, as in Henley-in-Arden, where many of the timber-framed houses of the 16th and 17th centuries survive to the present day; only the roofing materials have changed, from thatch to tile. Similarly, Shipston-on-Stour contains many stone-built houses erected in the first quarter of the 18th century. In other small towns, however, earlier timber and thatch dwellings were rebuilt in brick and tile in the 18th or early 19th centuries, or were re-faced with a new, fashionable brick front with sash windows. Atherstone and Coleshill are good examples of this sort of town. In Stratford-upon-Avon this process was hastened by the fires at the end of the 16th century. Thereafter, the Corporation insisted upon buildings on the street frontages having tiled roofs, so that fires spread less easily, and premises were regularly inspected and offenders fined. Fire caused even greater changes in Warwick, where a great conflagration swept through the town centre in 1694, destroying not only two of the principal streets, but also much of St Mary's Church. In the days before fire insurance, a charitable appeal was the only means of relief for those affected, and in Warwick some £11,000 was raised in this way. The Corporation also obtained a Fire Act setting up a body of commissioners to regulate the rebuilding. Under their control High Street was straightened, a small square was created before the church, and detailed regulations were laid down regarding the new houses. They had to be brick built, with tiled roofs and particular attention was paid to the three plots at the intersection of the four main streets which were to be 'built of equal height, the two first stories ten foot each, the third story eight foot high'. Cornices and pilasters completed the identical designs, while the undamaged Court House occupied the fourth corner. Warwick High Street remains one of the best early 18th century streets in the county as a result of this activity.

135 *18th-century fireman*

House Building

New cottages for the poorer classes were also built of brick and tile in the 18th century, usually simple one-up, one-down buildings perhaps with a scullery at the back. Once the main street frontages had been continuously built up, these cottages were provided in the back yards and gardens of larger houses and living conditions began to deteriorate markedly. This was especially so in Coventry, but by the early 19th century it was also a problem in Stratford and Warwick. In Stratford, the prosperity of the 1830s encouraged one landowner to develop a whole estate of these cottages to the south of the town centre, but with adequate space they are more attractive dwellings, have small back gardens and retain the vernacular brick and tile. The advent of the railways changed this vernacular tradition. Welsh roofing slates began to replace tiles, and machine-made, mass-produced bricks ousted the local hand-made variety. The later industrial housing of Coventry, Nuneaton, Bedworth and Rugby is therefore much less attractive.

136 *Fire insurance plate, Shipston-on-Stour*

House-building was a major industry in the 19th century, but building firms remained small and were often bankrupted in times of economic depression. Landowners and businessmen were more likely to survive with their greater financial resources and in Warwickshire perhaps the greatest and most successful speculation of all was the new town of Leamington Spa. At the beginning of the 19th century the spa was just one of a number in the West Midlands. Success depended upon good publicity and it was Leamington's good fortune to be blessed with some excellent publicists. By contrast, the incipient spa of Bishopton, just to the north of Stratford, where there was a higher quality of water, and where a consortium of local businessmen and landowners laid out roads, built a large hotel, a pump room and a church in the 1830s, simply failed to develop at all. At Leamington, James Bisset moved to the town in 1813 from Birmingham and opened an assembly room with a picture gallery, news room, and his 'Cabinet of Curiosities', a personally-assembled museum. This move was quickly followed by the publication of a *Guide* to the town, most of which was devoted to describing the delights of Bisset's own enterprises. The other factor in Leamington's favour was the quantity, as opposed to the quality, of its waters. After the construction of the Royal Pump Room in 1814 with its Boulton and Watt steam pump, the visitor could see his bath filled before his eyes, and thus be certain that it had been occupied by no-one before him, which was not always the case in other spas. Royal visits from the Prince Regent in 1819, and Princess Victoria in 1830, helped seal the reputation of the town, and in 1838 the new queen allowed the town to add the prestigious 'Royal' to its name.

Housing in the town was built in fits and starts, and local landowners were closely involved. The most important was probably Bertie Greathead of Guys Cliffe, just outside Warwick. It was he who began the development of the 'New Town' on the north bank of the river Leam in 1808. Other than the new pump room, the focus of this development was the great *Regent Hotel*, opened in 1819. As houses were erected and new shops opened in the new town, even more grandiose plans were prepared for the land to the north and east, the first by the London architect, P. F. Robinson, and the second by none other than John Nash. Many of the grand squares, terraces and villas planned by these architects never materialised because the developers were proceeding too quickly. In 1841, there were no fewer than 250 unoccupied houses in the town, about 10 per cent of the total, and it was not until the late 1850s that building began again in earnest. What had happened was that spas had gone out of fashion, and since most inhabitants leased their houses annually, rather than owning them, they simply moved elsewhere. Recovery was based on the fact that the town was a pleasant place in which to live. In the late 19th century, the inhabitants were the retired, widows, and prosperous middle-class residents moving out from Coventry, and the houses built for this group were detached suburban villas set back behind tree-filled gardens, rather than the urbane classicism of Robinson's terraces. Leamington became in effect a prestigious garden suburb.

Shopping Facilities

The evolution of shopping facilities in Warwickshire towns can be traced in some detail from 19th-century directories. In most smaller towns the number of inns, public houses and beer shops declined rapidly. In part this was a result of the demise of coaching, in part due to rationalisation in the brewing industry, and in part the result of evangelical campaigns against the evils of alcohol, which led first to licensing and then to closure of many beer shops and public houses. This is especially so in industrial Warwickshire with its strong Radical and Dissenting traditions which are reflected in the large number of nonconformist churches in the towns. Secondly, there is increasing reference to the general food store and a corresponding decline in the number of specialised food shops, though the appearance of greengrocers in the 1850s is an exception. Thirdly, professional services such as estate agents, solicitors, banks, and teachers increased substantially as the 19th century progressed, especially in Leamington, Rugby and Warwick where there was an above-average number of middle-class inhabitants. These three towns are especially noted, too, for the variety and number of their private schools in this period. Finally, the craft industries maintained and increased their significance as shoemakers, cabinet-makers, saddlers, stone masons, carpenters and such-like plied their trade in surrounding villages as well as in the towns. Clearly the highest quality shopping centre for a town of its size was Leamington. In the 1840s it could boast nearly a dozen booksellers, hairdressers, and wine merchants together with jewellers, silversmiths, silk merchants and tea dealers, and a score of surgeons and physicians to look after the spa visitors. In contrast Nuneaton had only eight surgeons for an equivalent population and few of the specialist shops. Here the lists are dominated by butchers, grocers, tailors, and shoemakers, and more than a hundred taverns and beer shops. One interesting addition to the services provided by most towns by the 1880s was a photographer (inevitably Leamington had several), who provided the sepia photographs of people and places which are such important source material for the later 19th century.

Living Standards

In the towns there was the same social contrast as in the countryside, but, except in Birmingham, rich and poor lived within sight of each other until the early 19th century. John Lucas, a Coventry wine merchant, lived in Broad Gate in 1790, in the very centre of the town. His large house, with five bedrooms, parlour, dining-room, kitchen, shop, cellars and garrets contained four-poster bedsteads; feather beds; quilts; mahogany chairs; dining, card and Pembroke tables; mirrors; chests of drawers, and Wilton carpets. Cellars were important for the better-off as ale, beer and cider could be stored and the diet of this group was varied in the extreme. The Birmingham historian and bookseller, William Hutton, had sugar, various teas, coffee, a great variety of spices, preserved fruits—including apricots and quinces—pickled walnuts and mushrooms, bottled shrimps, and other such luxuries in his store cupboards in the 1790s.

For ordinary townspeople, life was more severe and they lived mainly on bread, bacon and potatoes. In Birmingham, in the 1840s, 'cook-shops' provided the working man with his dinner at fourpence for a plate of meat and potatoes, and soup was a penny per pint, but urban living conditions were at their worst. Poorly-built, two- or three-storey houses were built back-to-back around badly-drained courtyards with shared privies at one end. Rents were between two and four shillings per week. Infant mortality was appallingly high; nearly half of all deaths in the 1830s were of children under five years of age as

137 *Baroque doorway, Temple Row, Birmingham, c.1790*

138 *No.2 Court, Allison Street, Birmingham, 1905. A broad, well-paved courtyard of back-to-back houses probably built in the 1850s. Note the water standpipe and single privy to serve the whole court*

measles, scarlet fever and pneumonia took their toll. Both Coventry an Birmingham escaped the worst of the cholera epidemics of the mid-19t century, though there was an outbreak in the Coventry workhouse in 183 which caused some fifty deaths in a fortnight. Industrial accidents were continuing hazard and clothing or hair was frequently trapped in unguarde machinery causing terrible injuries. Wages varied greatly, but on average boy of 13 or 14 might earn four shillings a week; by the age of 20 they could ear 13 or 14 shillings; and as adults about £1 5s. 0d. Girls and women normall were paid only half the male wage.

Entertainments in both town and country for the mass of people wer relatively simple. Bull-baiting and cock-fighting were popular in 18th-centur Birmingham, while prize-fighting was also growing in popularity. By th mid-century cricket and football were also coming to the fore. For th gentry, racing, hunting, shooting and archery were popular, and 'beating th bushes' often provided extra income for schoolboys. Even in 1900, the teache at Elmdon school recorded that 'attendance very poor this week owing t boys being away bush-beating'. Similar excuses for school absence include pea-picking and currant gathering in June at Weston-on-Avon, guardin field mushrooms for a farmer in Henley-in-Arden, and gleaning after th harvest in most villages. The return of older girls 'in service' for their annua holiday was another such occasion. At Brailes a regular log book entry i mid-October during the 1870s was 'not so many children—sisters home fo holidays'.

The Rise of Birmingham

In the mid-16th century Birmingham was a medium-sized town with perhap 1,500 inhabitants but, as its iron-working trades began to develop, the town too, began to expand rapidly. By 1650 its population was probably roun 5,000, so that it was easily the largest town on the plateau, though stil rather smaller than Coventry. At this time it was still basically a timber-buil town. The smith's workshops were concentrated along the streets of Deriten and Digbeth on either side of the river Rea, while the commercial heart o the town was just to the north around the triangular Bull Ring marke place, with the parish church of St Martins in the middle, and the ol moated manor of the de Birmingham family to the south. Beyond the Bul Ring, the town was expanding up on to the plateau top along 'High Town' the later High Street. During the 18th century Birmingham quickly over took Coventry as the largest town in Warwickshire. By 1720, there wer more than 11,000 inhabitants; by the middle of the century, nearly 24,00 by 1780, some 50,000; and at the first census, nearly 74,000 people lived i Birmingham, Edgbaston and Aston. Until the later 19th century these latte two places remained administratively separate from Birmingham.

Such rapid growth meant great changes in the physical appearance of th town. It was sustained by the variety of metal-manufacturing trades whic wreathed the town in smoke, fumes and noise. As one contemporary observe

declared, it was 'not a place a gentleman would choose to make a residence. Its continual noise and smoke prevent it from being desirable in that respect', while among other disadvantages were 'its close population, the noxious effusion of various metallic trades and above all the continual smoke arising from the immense quantity of coals consumed'. Much of the early growth of industry and population was accommodated within courts of cottages and workshops built on the 'backsides' of existing houses, so that the older streets became a congested tangle of alleys and courtyards of insanitary housing. However, new streets were also being built. Bull Street, Dale End, New Street, and Moor Street had all been added by 1700, and by 1731 a further 23 new streets were chronicled and there were estimated to be over 3,700 houses in the town. Some developments were of quite high quality. In 1713, one of the town's merchants, a Mr. Pemberton, laid out an elegant tree-lined square of houses to the north of Bull Street designed by William Westley. This Old Square was matched by an even grander layout between Bull Street and New Street, where, from 1711, Thomas Archer's Baroque St Philip's church was being built because St Martin's 'could not contain the great part of the inhabitants'. By the mid-1720s the 'lofty, elegant and uniform' terraces of Temple Row and the square around the new church were being built for 'people of fortune, who were great wholesale dealers in the manufactures of this town'.

In the second half of the 18th century new streets and houses continued to spread north, east and west of the older part of the town. Much of this

139 *St Philip's Church, Birmingham, 1732. Thomas Archer's Baroque church, now the cathedral, was consecrated in 1715. The churchyard was surrounded by elegant Georgian houses for merchants in the tradition begun in Old Square (see inset).*

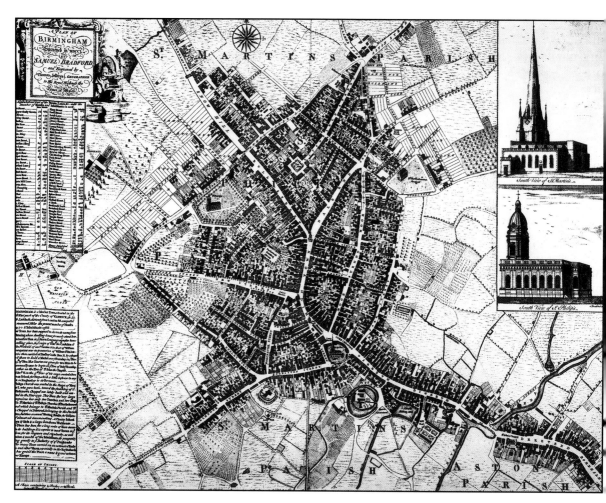

140 *Bradford's plan of Birmingham, 1750. Samuel Bradford's plan of the city was the second to be published. It shows The Moat, Birmingham's manor house, the crowded Bull Ring market place and the new streets laid out on the Colmore estate north west of St Philip's*

development took place on the New Hall estate of the Colmore family. From 1746, the Colmores slowly developed a grid of streets about the central axis of Newhall Street. Building plots were let on 120-year leases, and some attempt was made to specify the type and value of property erected. In 1779, St Paul's church was completed, standing four-square in a well-planted churchyard which was intended to be the focus of the next phase of development, the Colmores themselves having given £1,000 towards the cost of the church. The majority of the inhabitants of these new houses were small manufacturers only too anxious to abandon the unhealthy over-crowding of Digbeth and Deritend as soon as they could afford to do so. Their new 'good substantial dwelling houses with the proper and necessary outbuildings' were graceful, three-storey, Georgian brick houses. Unfortunately, the nature of Birmingham's workshop industries meant that many of these small manufacturers were not yet in a position to separate home from workplace. Back gardens were therefore often speedily built over

with industrial premises and cottages for their workmen, while even the
upper rooms of the principal house were often used as workshop space.
Inevitably, too, not all of the new houses being put up were of as high
quality as those around St Paul's Square. Such was the demand for
accommodation that builders found it quite easy to sell poorly-built houses
using the cheapest materials and, by the early years of the 19th century, the
town was ringed by close-built developments of narrow, ill-ventilated courtyards of insanitary housing.

Birmingham Industries

The nature of Birmingham's industries changed somewhat from the early
18th century. Though the smiths, grinders, cutters and tanners could still be
found around the lower end of the town, the manufacture of small metal
goods, buttons, guns, jewellery and brass articles came increasingly to
dominate. These new industries emphasised the application of a relatively
high degree of skill to a limited amount of raw material to give a high value
product; important in an inland manufacturing centre where transport costs
were high. They also emphasised an extreme division of labour. Gun-making
is a good example of such a trade. This industry developed in Birmingham

141 *St Paul's church,
Birmingham*

142 *Steel pen works,
Birmingham, c.1820. A
typical 'toy' factory with
narrow street frontage
and workshops around a
courtyard. The steam
engine in the yard was
used to power machinery
in the works*

143 *Matthew Boulton, engineer and manufacturer*

from the 1690s when 'musquets' cost 17s. each. As British colonial trade and the size of the army, expanded in the 18th century so did the demand for Birmingham guns. For weapons of the highest quality as many as fifty separate craftsmen could be involved, ranging from barrel and stock makers, to barrel grinders, lock makers, carvers, engravers and wadding makers. This multiplicity of crafts led to the concentration of gun firms in one part of the city, focused on Loveday Street and St Mary's Row, east of Snow Hill. In 1813 the town acquired its own Gun Proof House where barrels were tested and approved since by this time Birmingham gun-makers were supplying about two-thirds of the firearms used by the army and navy.

Other trades were organised in much the same way. Button- and buckle-making and the bewildering variety of the 'toy' trade all relied on specialist craftsmen and a variety of metals, from brass and steel to precious metals and alloys, but it is perhaps the jewellery trade, which emerged towards the end of the 18th century, that most closely compares with the gun trade. Jewellers, too, concentrated in one area of the city, around St Paul's church-yard, most of them being their own masters with perhaps an apprentice or their wives and children to help out. By the mid-19th century the centre of the jewellery quarter had shifted northwards to Great Hampton Street and by the 1870s had reached its present location around Vyse Street. Again, there was a remarkable division of crafts, including polishing, cutting, engraving, setting, enamelling, traders in precious stones, and even men who made a living collecting scrapings of gold and silver for subsequent re-use. Some 3,700 people were employed in the jewellery trade in 1845.

There were other types of industrial organisation, however, and from the mid-18th century factories were introduced. The first was probably John Taylor's button and snuffbox manufactory in Dale End, where four or five hundred workers were employed. There was heavy investment in machinery and division of labour to speed up the manufacturing process. It also allowed women and children to be employed for many of the simple and repetitive jobs. In the button industry generally, for example, of the 6,000 people employed in 1865, some two-thirds were women and children. In 1765, John Taylor, with Samson Lloyd, used some of his profits to help found Birmingham's first bank, an enterprise which outlasted the manufactory since it was the predecessor of today's Lloyds Bank, Plc. Other important early factories included John Baskerville's japanning business at Easy Hill, though he, too, is better known today for his much-used typeface, rather than his factory, and Matthew Boulton's Soho Works. Boulton began as a buckle- and button-maker, but after opening the works in 1764 founded a national reputation for his jewellery, silver and plated table ware. The Works was intended to bring the costs of manufacture as low as possible, but the goods produced were of the highest quality design and workmanship and were marketed nationally. In the 1770s he went into partnership with James Watt, and in 1796 a new works, the Soho Factory, was opened to manufacture steam engines. A little later William Murdock's development of gas for lighting purposes provided a second major product for the Foundry. Many

144 *James Watt*

of the factories were built close to the developing canal network so that raw materials could be brought in cheaply. Indeed, many factories had short branch canals coming right into the centre of the factory premises. By the 1820s the canals ringed Birmingham on all sides but the south, and this canal ring is the artery of a similar belt of close-built industrial premises around the centre of the city.

Suburban Development

These industrialists, together with the most prosperous solicitors, land agents, and other professional men were among the first to move right out of the city when they looked for somewhere to live. Beyond the canals and industry in the early 19th century, Birmingham was surrounded by a broad belt of garden land which supplied the city with fruit, vegetables and milk. Beyond these gardens, hamlets such as Camp Hill, Bordesley and Islington were being developed by enterprising landowners and builders with detached ornamental villas and short terraces of stuccoed houses for the professional classes. These first generation suburbs were quickly swamped by the expanding city and by the 1850s villages further out from the centre, such as Moseley, King's Heath, Harborne, Erdington, and Handsworth were being developed

145 *Birmingham Bull Ring, 1827. St Martin's parish church stood in the midst of the triangular Bull Ring market place. From High Street this view looks out over the busy market stalls with Nelson's statue in the centre looking towards Digbeth and Camp Hill*

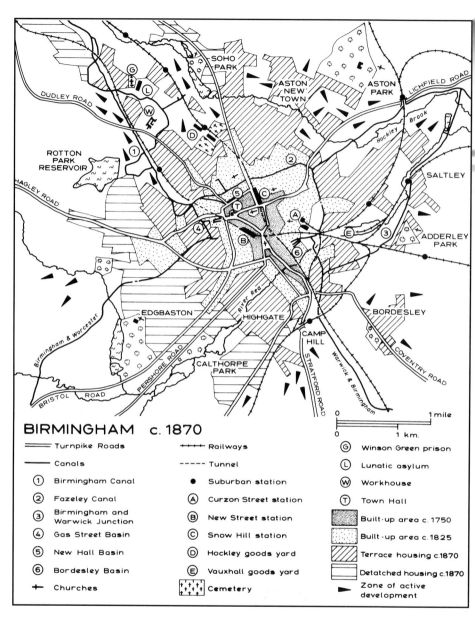

BIRMINGHAM c. 1870

═══ Turnpike Roads	┼┼┼┼ Railways	Ⓖ Winson Green prison
─── Canals	----- Tunnel	Ⓛ Lunatic asylum
① Birmingham Canal	● Suburban station	Ⓦ Workhouse
② Fazeley Canal	Ⓐ Curzon Street station	Ⓣ Town Hall
③ Birmingham and Warwick Junction	Ⓑ New Street station	Built-up area c.1750
④ Gas Street Basin	Ⓒ Snow Hill station	Built-up area c.1825
⑤ New Hall Basin	Ⓓ Hockley goods yard	Terrace housing c.1870
⑥ Bordesley Basin	Ⓔ Vauxhall goods yard	Detached housing c.1870
✝ Churches	Cemetery	► Zone of active development

146 *Birmingham in c.1870*

in the same way. Many landowners tried to establish their particular housing development as the most prestigious in the city, but all but one were eventually overtaken by Birmingham's inexorable expansion. Only to the west, where the whole manor of Edgbaston was under the control of the Gough-Calthorpe family, who refused to allow the building of factories and warehouses, did high-quality housing remain high status throughout the 19th and, indeed, the 20th centuries.

Birmingham's population became increasingly segregated into distinct social areas as the 19th century progressed, the detached mansions of Edgbaston contrasting markedly with both the densely packed courts of the inner city, and the rectangular street pattern and monotonous rows of terraced housing provided for artisan workers in the later 19th century in areas such as Aston, Saltley, and Small Heath. In comparison with other great industrial cities, Birmingham was well-built and reasonably healthy even in the dark days of the 1830s and 1840s. However, in the town centre the enclosed courts of back-to-back houses often had rudimentary sanitary arrangements, poor or non-existent drainage, and inadequate water supply. As well as scores of people, these courts also housed dogs and pigs, which added to the problems. There were no less than 3,210 pigs in the borough in 1845!

Government and Institutions

This rapidly-growing city was administered by manorial and parochial officials until a Charter of Incorporation raised it to borough status in 1838. Since the manor and parish officers served on a part-time and honorary basis it is not surprising that by the 1760s the system was totally inadequate. Law and order was the responsibility of two constables and the 'head borough', while there were only four surveyors to look after the ever-expanding road system. Inevitably, salaried officials were required. Poor law administration was transferred from the parish vestry to a Board of Guardians in 1783, and, rather earlier, in 1768, the leading citizens of the town had petitioned Parliament for an Improvement Act. Under this Act a body of 'Commissioners of the Streets' was established with powers to levy a rate for cleaning and lighting the streets, removing obstructive buildings and building a new cattle market. Subsequent Acts enabled the Commissioners to establish a body of night watchmen to police the town, and to build a number of much-needed public buildings. Other public services were provided by the initiative and generosity of individuals, philanthropic organisations and the churches. A general hospital was provided in 1779, funded by a variety of schemes which included the town's famous triennial Music Festivals. Eye, fever and other hospitals followed in the early 19th century. Education was provided by the old-established King Edward's School, by the Blue Coat School, opened in 1724, and by a variety of church-sponsored charity schools, by the National schools of the Church of England, and by the British schools of the nonconformists. There were also the Sunday schools which were built in large numbers in the early 19th century. Other social facilities included the Theatre Royal 'one of the most superb theatres out of the Metropolis', and the town hall, opened as an assembly and concert hall in 1834 to the designs of Joseph Hansom.

Birmingham became a County Borough in 1889, a city in 1896, and by 1911 a series of boundary extensions had enclosed Aston, Handworth, King's Norton, Northfield, Yardley, and Erdington into the administrative purview of the city. During the second half of the 19th century one man towers over

147 *Rt. Hon. Joseph Chamberlain, M.P.*

148 *Corporation Street, Birmingham, 1899. This new thoroughfare was laid out between 1878 and 1882 due to the initiative of Joseph Chamberlain. Viewed from New Street the buildings are little changed today but traffic and fashions are very different*

the local government of the city—Joseph Chamberlain. He was elected to the council in 1869 and became mayor in 1873. Over the next three years he presided over the most ambitious improvement schemes outside London. In 1874 his scheme for the purchase of the town's two gas companies was approved, and within two years produced both a substantial profit for the town and prices which were 30 per cent lower for consumers. The following year the water company was also taken into municipal ownership. Chamberlain's third great scheme involved clearing some of the town's worst slums and providing a grand new thoroughfare for the city-centre in the shape of Corporation Street. This great Improvement Area scheme of 93 acres was carried forward under the Artisans' and Labourers' Dwellings Act of 1875. Work began on demolishing poor housing and laying out the new street in 1878. By 1882, Corporation Street had reached its junction with Aston Street. The initial cost was met from the profits of the gas undertaking and from the rents received from leasing the new properties along the street. By 1892 it was paying for itself. At the New Street end,

Corporation Street rapidly became the most fashionable of the city shopping streets, with department stores, smaller shops, restaurants, coffee houses, the Cobden temperance hotel, a theatre, two arcades, and a winter gardens. At the Aston Street end the new Victoria Law Courts, opened in 1891 and designed in brilliant terracotta by Aston Webb and Ingress Bell, provide a fitting termination to the new street. Joseph Chamberlain became a Member of Parliament in 1876, but continued to take a close interest in the affairs of the city. Corporation Street and the recently-restored commemorative fountain in Chamberlain Square are fitting memorials to a great man.

149   *City of Birmingham arms*

10

Warwickshire, 1900-1995

Through the 20th century the urbanised northern and central parts of War wickshire have enjoyed almost unrivalled prosperity and growth, while since 1945 this prosperity has extended to the more rural parts of the shire. In terms of population even the smaller towns have doubled in size since 1901 In the west, Alcester has increased from 2,300 to 4,600, to the south, Southam has grown from 1,800 to 4,400 inhabitants, and to the north Coleshill ha expanded from 2,600 to 6,300. More significantly, many of the medium sized towns have shown a similar rate of growth—Warwick from 12,000 to 18,000, and Leamington from 26,000 to 45,000, while the population o Birmingham has also nearly doubled to over one million inhabitants. More spectacular has been the growth of Kenilworth from 4,500 to over 20,000 of Rugby from 17,000 to nearly 60,000, of Bedworth from 7,000 to 40,000 and the most rapid growth of all in Coventry, where modern industry provided work for an extra quarter million inhabitants, and in Solihull where the small town of less than 8,000 people in 1901 is now a metropolitan region of over 100,000 people. The growth of many of the smaller towns, as well as of the villages, in the north and central parts of the county is very much dependent upon the industrial and commercial prosperity of Birmingham and Coventry, and upon the widespread ownership of motor cars which commenced in the 1950s and 1960s. Many of the new inhabitants of Stratford Kenilworth and Leamington work elsewhere, while the very rapid growth o Solihull is mainly a result of Birmingham overspilling its boundaries.

Such a rapidly changing distribution of population has meant that loca government administration has also had to change, and, in 1974, new county and district boundaries were drawn. Birmingham, Solihull, Coventry, and the rural strip of country around Meriden were removed from Warwickshire and combined with the Black Country towns of south Staffordshire to form a new County of the West Midlands. The remainder of the old shire, excepting a small area of Tamworth which was joined to Staffordshire, survives as a new county of Warwickshire. The new county is divided into five large distric council areas, while the former Warwickshire part of the West Midland forms another three metropolitan districts. The West Midlands county survived for only 12 years and plans for further local government reorganisation are on the table once more in 1995. The regional, town and district planning for

150 *Humberette car, 1914*

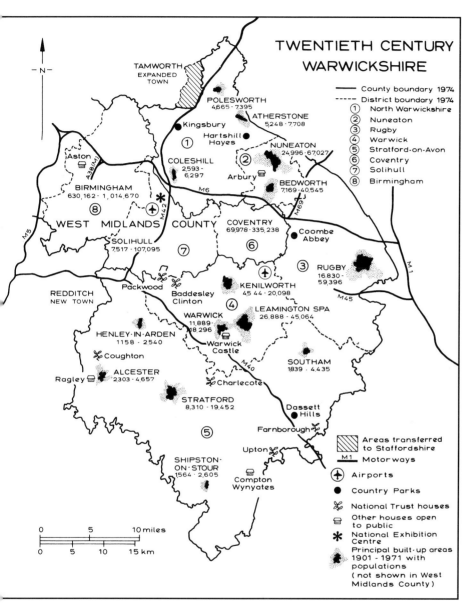

TWENTIETH CENTURY
WARWICKSHIRE

——— County boundary 1974
- - - - District boundary 1974
① North Warwickshire
② Nuneaton
③ Rugby
④ Warwick
⑤ Stratford-on-Avon
⑥ Coventry
⑦ Solihull
⑧ Birmingham

TAMWORTH
EXPANDED
TOWN

POLESWORTH
4,665 - 7,395

ATHERSTONE
5,248 - 7,708

Kingsbury

Hartshill
Hayes

NUNEATON
24,996 - 67,027

①

COLESHILL
2,593 -
6,297

Arbury

②

BEDWORTH
7,169 - 40,545

Aston
A38(M)

BIRMINGHAM
630,162 - 1,014,670

⑧

M6

WEST MIDLANDS COUNTY

M42

*

COVENTRY
69,978 - 335,238

M69

Coombe
Abbey

SOLIHULL
7,517 - 107,095

⑦

⑥

③ RUGBY
16,830 -
59,396

M5

Packwood

Baddesley
Clinton

KENILWORTH
45.44 - 20,098

④

M1

M45

REDDITCH
NEW TOWN

LEAMINGTON SPA
26,888 - 45,064

WARWICK
11,889 -
18,296

HENLEY-IN-ARDEN
1158 - 2540

Coughton

Warwick
Castle

SOUTHAM
1839 - 4.435

M40

Ragley

ALCESTER
2303 - 4,657

Charlecote

STRATFORD
8,310 - 19,452

Dassett
Hills

⑤

Farnborough

Upton

SHIPSTON-
ON-STOUR
1564 - 2,605

Compton
Wynyates

0   5   10 miles
0 5   10   15 km

Areas transferred
to Staffordshire
M1 Motorways
⊕ Airports
● Country Parks
⚘ National Trust houses
⌂ Other houses open
to public
* National Exhibition
Centre
Principal built-up areas
1901 - 1971 with
populations
(not shown in West
Midlands County)

151 *20th-century*
Warwickshire

which these local authorities are responsible is very much a phenomenon of
the 20th century, though its roots can be traced back into the later 19th
century, when municipal councils acquired responsibility for paving, lighting,
sewerage, public health, and, in some instances, for gas, water, and slum
clearance. The Birmingham council had to concern itself especially with water-
supply because of the watershed location of the city. In 1891, they approved
the construction of reservoirs in the Elan valley in mid-Wales with a 73-mile-
long aqueduct to bring water to holding reservoirs on the city's outskirts.

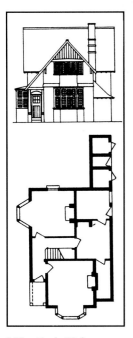

152 *Early 20th-century house, Bournville*

153 *The University of Birmingham*

The improvement of existing housing and the provision of new housing has been the concern of all local authorities since 1919. In Birmingham alone at that time, some 200,000 people were housed in back-to-back dwellings in the central districts grouped around 'dark, insanitary and badly lit courts'. Over 42,000 houses in the city had no separate water supply, and more than 58,000 were without their own sanitation. Houses were over-crowded, since house-building had failed to keep pace with population growth, and factories, workshops and warehouses were distributed through these inner housing areas. There were similar problems in the older areas of Coventry, Nuneaton, Stratford, and Warwick. In the 1920s and '30s the solution to these housing problems was much influenced by the garden city ideal and council-built houses were erected in semi-detached pairs, at modest densities, with substantial gardens and served by cursive geometrical street patterns. Speculative private builders were supplying slightly larger houses in other districts, normally with simpler road grids. The result of this building activity is that all of the larger towns are characterised by extensive, low-density housing estates of this inter war period which enormously increased the areal spread of the towns. These estates are also exclusively residential since the new planning powers enabled housing and industry to be directed to different districts.

Two of the pioneers who initiated the changed attitude to housing are associated with Birmingham. Between 1893 and 1899, George Cadbury assembled an estate beside his suburban chocolate factory at Bournville and began to create a new 'village' of cheap, well-built houses in an attractive environment. The houses were not reserved for his employees and in 1900 Cadbury created the Bournville Village Trust to manage the community which by that time consisted of some 800 families. The brick houses were constructed in groups of up to four. Gardens were large, streets were tree lined, there were extensive parks and recreational facilities, and the village centre had shops, church and schools. A second Birmingham industrialist, J.S. Nettlefold, was instrumental in initiating an estate similar to Bournville at Harborne. This was run by an association of the tenants and again the attractive houses are laid out along tree-lined roads with a central community building, shops and tennis courts.

Post-1945 planning combined the demolition of inner-city slums in Birmingham and Coventry with further extensive housing developments at the urban fringe. A new feature of both the clearance areas and the new estates, especially from 1960 onwards, has been the point block of flats. Birmingham, which had previously had very few flat blocks more than three or four storeys high, became a city of towers within a decade. The reduction in housing densities meant that urban areas continued to expand and some of Birmingham's overspill population and industry was directed right away from the city to new or expanded towns at Telford, Redditch and Tamworth. There were also new peripheral estates, often up to ten miles from the city centre at, for example, Chelmsley Wood, with housing for 50,000 people.

The city centres of both Coventry and Birmingham have been substantially rebuilt since 1945. In Birmingham, the city's Chief Engineer, Herbert

Manzoni, was particularly influential in initiating new fast roads around the town centre and the rebuilding of extensive areas of the commercial heart, including the enclosed shopping centre at the Bull Ring. At Coventry the rebuilding was necessitated by the devastating air raid on 14-15 November 1940, which destroyed much of the city centre, including the cathedral. Plans for rebuilding were put into effect immediately after the war, and the modern shopping centre is largely pedestrianised. The centre-piece of the scheme is Sir Basil Spence's new cathedral, opened in 1962 and set at right-angles to the ruins of the old, which form an integral part of it. The cathedral, with its huge tapestry, magnificent stained glass, statuary and modern furnishings, immediately became Warwickshire's most famous 20th-century building, and is a worthy successor to the medieval splendour of St Michael's.

The doyen of British planners, Sir Patrick Abercrombie, provided a plan for the development of Warwick in 1949. Its conclusions were not followed and Warwick suffered the indignity of the slab of County Council offices which ruins the visual prospect of the town from the north. By the late 1960s people began to demand the preservation of historic townscapes and villages and conservation rather than redevelopment came to the fore. Many town centres were pedestrianised in the 1970s and '80s but, surprisingly, not Stratford-on-Avon with its tourist throngs, though plans were made in 1967.

Alterations to the transport network have wrought dramatic changes in the Warwickshire landscape and in the lives of its inhabitants. The first of several revolutions was the revival of road transport at the beginning of the century. An era of cheap public transport was ushered in, first by the electric tram and then by the development of the motor bus. Without this change, the cities could not have expanded so dramatically and homes could not have been separated from workplace. In the countryside frequent bus services were a boon, but they provided an easy means for young villagers to seek their fortune in the prospering industries of the larger towns so that the populations of some rural communities began to decline. This was particularly so after 1945 when the mechanisation of agriculture reduced the size of the agricultural workforce. The private motor car brought new changes, and by the 1960s rural bus services were being closed, and the motor car enabled the better-off to return to the villages to live, while continuing to work in the cities and larger towns.

Commercial traffic, too, switched to the roads, so that today the canal system is used exclusively for pleasure boating, and the majority of the rural railway network has been closed and the tracks removed. To cope with the ever-increasing numbers of cars and lorries on the roads new highways have had to be built, and the West Midlands has found itself once more at the hub of a national network, in this instance the motorways. The M6 traverses the northern half of the county and as it passes through Birmingham provides another, less attractive, 20th-century monument of first rank—the multi-level interchange at Gravelly Hill which was affectionately christened Spaghetti Junction. The M42 rings Birmingham to the east and south through attractive countryside preserved by the West Midlands Green Belt, and the M40 now

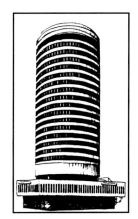

154 *The Rotunda, Birmingham*

bisects Warwickshire and has brought new economic pressures for development along its length. The railway stations at Coventry and Birmingham New Street were rebuilt in the 1960s while a new station was provided to serve Birmingham airport and the National Exhibition Centre. There is an inland container port in Birmingham for rail freight traffic. Birmingham airport at Elmdon provides international services, and has been substantially enlarged in the 1980s.

The motor industry was the basis of the 20th-century prosperity of the West Midlands. There are large assembly plants at Longbridge, Solihull and Coventry, while the component firms making engines, tyres and electrical fittings still employ thousands more people. However, from 1970 the motor industry began to disintegrate in the face of foreign competition. By 1980 the problem was acute and unemployment in parts of Birmingham and Coventry reached 20 per cent. Only Liverpool suffered a greater economic decline. The 1980s and '90s have seen some improvement as Birmingham, in particular, has attracted office employment and has become a business tourist centre. The opening of the International Convention Centre in 1990, and the transformation of the city centre with pedestrianisation, fountains and public art have brought in new service industry employment. The retail industry has also brought transformations in the 1980s to towns in all parts of the county. Large edge-of-town supermarkets and retail parks, with extensive car parks, now characterise Stratford, Leamington, Rugby, Solihull and Coventry, whilst new housing developments continue to expand the size of country towns.

Despite this, Warwickshire also remains an agricultural county of the first rank. Pastoral farming continued to dominate until the 1950s, but then pastures were increasingly ploughed up for cereal production. 'Factory' farming of pigs and poultry is important in north Warwickshire, and vegetable crops are significant in the south-west. The National Vegetable Research Station was established at Wellesbourne, near Stratford, which itself houses the headquarters of the National Farmers' Union. The Royal Agricultural Society's permanent show ground has been developed at Stoneleigh and new wholesale fruit and vegetable markets in the centre of Birmingham are among the most modern in the country. Tourism has been important in Warwickshire since the 18th century and is today a significant industry. Warwick Castle is among the most visited of all English country houses, still more so since its potential has been developed by Madam Tussauds, and Coughton Court is one of the most popular of the National Trust's houses. More unexpected is the rapid development of business tourism in Birmingham, but the magnet for most tourist visitors to the county remains the home town of its most famous son—William Shakespeare's Stratford-upon-Avon.

155 *William Shakespeare's monument, Holy Trinity, Stratford*

Select Bibliography

This bibliography is a brief guide to the extensive literature on the history of Warwickshire, Coventry and Birmingham. It is not a list of works consulted in writing this book. Articles of interest only to the specialist are excluded, but some periodical literature is noted because it represents the only written material on certain topics.

The Victoria History of the County of Warwick is the principal reference work for the county's history, and, in contrast with many counties, has been completed. Volume I (1904) contains sections on prehistory, archaeology and Domesday Book. Volume II (1908) has articles on religious history and institutions, schools, sport, political history and industrial pursuits. Volumes III-IV (1947-51) describe the history of all the parishes in the four hundreds: Barlichway, Hemlingford, Kingston, and Knightlow. Volume VII (1964) contains a history of Birmingham, and Volume VIII (1965) histories of Coventry and Warwick.

A number of societies exist for the publication of articles concerned with the history and archaeology of the county and for the publication of documents. The most important, with the date of first publication, are: *Birmingham Archaeological Society Transactions* (1870). This became the Birmingham and Warwickshire Archaeological Society in 1965. The Society publishes material on the history and archaeology of Birmingham, Warwickshire and the West Midlands region.

University of Birmingham Historical Journal (1947). This became *Midland History* in 1971, and publishes scholarly articles on the history of the West Midland region.

Warwickshire History (1969). The journal of the Warwickshire Local History Society, who also publish Occasional Papers.

Dugdale Society Publications (1921). These contain transcriptions, with scholarly introductions, of historical records relating to Warwickshire. The Society also publishes a series of *Occasional Papers* (1924). In addition, the Coventry branch of the Historical Association has published a series of *Coventry and North Warwickshire History Pamphlets* and some local history societies have enterprising Newsletters and Occasional Papers, notably the Alcester and District Local History Society. The Birmingham and Midland Society for Genealogy and Heraldry publishes *The Midland Ancestor*.

Warwickshire

Abercrombie, P. and Nickson, R., *Warwick, its preservation and redevelopment* (Warwick, 1949)

Alcock, N., *People at Home. Living in a Warwickshire Village, 1550-1800* (Chichester, 1993)

Banks, F.R., *Warwickshire and the Shakespeare country* (London, 1960)

Barnes, E.E., *The rise of the Midland Railway 1844-1874* (London, 1966)

Bedford, W.K.R., *History of Sutton Coldfield* (Birmingham, 1891)

Beresford, M.W., 'Deserted villages of Warwickshire' in *Birmingham Archaeological Society Transactions 66* (1950)

Booth, P., *Roman Alcester* (Stratford, 1981)

Bracken, L., *History of the Forest and Chase of Sutton Coldfield* (London, 1860)

Broadbridge, S.R., *The Birmingham Canal Navigations, 1768-1846* (Newton Abbot, 1974)

Brook, F., *The Industrial archaeology of the British Isles I: the West Midlands* (London, 1977)

Christiansen, R., *A regional history of the railways of Great Britain 7: The West Midlands* (Newton Abbot, 1973)

Cooper, W., *Wootton Wawen, its history and records* (Leeds, 1936)

Cooper, W., *Henley in Arden: an ancient market town and its surroundings* (Birmingham, 1946)

Cossons, A., 'Warwickshire turnpikes' in *Birmingham Archaeological Society Transactions 64* (1946)

Darby, H.C. and Terrett, I.B. (eds.), *The Domesday geography of Midland England* (Cambridge, 1954)

Dugdale, Sir W., *The antiquities of Warwickshire illustrated* (London, 1656)

Evershed, H., 'Farming of Warwickshire' in *Journal of Royal Agricultural Society of England 17* (1856)

Field, W., *An historical and descriptive account of the town and castle of Warwick* (Warwick, 1815)

Fogg, N., *Stratford upon Avon. Portrait of a town* (Chichester, 1986)

Forrest, H.E., *The old houses of Stratford-upon-Avon* (London, 1925)

Fox, L., *The borough town of Stratford-upon-Avon* (Stratford, 1953)

Gardner, S.M. and Ibbotson, E.M.H., *The history of Ilmington* (Stratford, 1974)

Gelling, M., *The West Midlands in the Early Middle Ages* (Leicester, 1992)

Gill, C., *Studies in Midland History* (Oxford, 1930)

Gooder, A., *Plague and enclosure, a Warwickshire village in the 17th century* (Clifton-upon-Dunsmore) (1965)

Gover, J.E.B., Mawer, A. and Stenton, F.M., *The place-names of Warwickshire* (Cambridge, 1936)

Hadfield, C., *The canals of the West Midlands* (Newton Abbot, 1966)

Hadfield, C. and Norris, J., *Waterways to Stratford* (Newton Abbot, 1962)

Hannett, J., *The Forest of Arden, its towns, villages and hamlets* (London, 1863)

Harris, M.D., *Some manors, churches and villages of Warwickshire* (Coventry, 1937)

Hooke, D., *The Anglo-Saxon Landscape. The Kingdom of the Hwicce* (Manchester, 1985)

Hudson, R., *Memorials of a Warwickshire parish: Lapworth* (London, 1904)

Hughes, A., *Politics, Society and Civil War in Warwickshire, 1620-1660* (Cambridge, 1987)

Kemp, T., *A history of Warwick and its people* (Warwick, 1905)

Kinvig, R.H., Smith, J.G. and Wise, M.J., *Birmingham and its regional setting* (Birmingham, 1950)

Lloyd, T.H., 'Royal Leamington Spa' in *Middle class housing in Britain*, eds. M.A. Simpson and T.H. Lloyd (Newton Abbot, 1977)

McPherson, A.W., *The land of Britain: Warwickshire* (London, 1946)

Morris, J. (ed.), *Domesday Book: Warwickshire* (Chichester, 1976)

Pevsner, N. and Wedgwood, A., *The buildings of England: Warwickshire* (London, 1966)

Reid, P.M., *Burkes and Savills guide to country houses II: Warwickshire etc.* (London, 1980)

Roberts, B.K., 'Field systems of the West Midlands' in *Studies of field systems in the British Isles*, eds. A.R.H. Baker and R.A. Butlin (Cambridge, 1973)

Rowlands, M.B., *Masters and men in the West Midland metalware trades before the Industrial Revolution* (Manchester, 1975)

Sherwood, R., *The Civil War in the Midlands 1642-1651* (Stroud, 1992)

Skipp, V.H.T., *Discovering Bickenhill* (Birmingham, 1963)

Skipp, V.H.T., *Crisis and development 1570-1674* (Cambridge, 1978)

Slater, T.R. and Jarvis, P.J. (eds.), *Field and forest: an historical geography of Warwickshire and Worcestershire* (Norwich, 1981)

Styles, P., *Studies in 17th century West Midland history* (Kineton, 1976)

Tate, W.E., 'Enclosure Acts and Awards relating to Warwickshire' in *Birmingham Archaeological Society Transactions 65* (1949)

Tennant, P., *Edgehill and beyond. The People's War in the South Midlands, 1642-1645* (Stroud, 1992)

Thomas, N., 'An archaeological gazetteer for Warwickshire: Neolithic to Iron Age', in *Birmingham and Warwickshire Archaeological Society 86* (1974)

Thorpe, H., 'The lord and the landscape' in *Birmingham Archaeological Society Transactions 80* (1965)

Timmins, S., *Birmingham and the Midland Hardware district* (London, 1866)

Tyack, G., *Warwickshire Country Houses* (Chichester, 1994)

Woodall, J., *From Hroca to Anne, being a 1,000 years in the life of Rowington* (Solihull, 1974)

Birmingham

Bickley, W.B. (ed.), *Survey of Birmingham, 1553* (Birmingham, 1886)

Bournville Village Trust, *When we build again* (London, 1941)

Bunce, J. T., *A history of the Birmingham General Hospital and the musical festivals* (Birmingham, 1873)

Chinn, C., *Homes for People, 100 years of Council Housing in Birmingham* (Exeter, 1991)

Gill, C., *History of Birmingham of 1865* (Oxford, 1952)

Harris, C., *The history of the Birmingham gun barrel Proof House* (Birmingham, 1946)

Hutton, W., *An history of Birmingham* (Birmingham, 1783)

Langford, J.A., *A century of Birmingham life* (Birmingham, 1870-1)

Little, B., *Birmingham buildings* (Newton Abbot, 1971)

Lloyd, S., *The Lloyds of Birmingham* (Birmingham, 1907)

Skipp, V.H.T., *A history of greater Birmingham down to 1830* (Birmingham, 1980)

Tann, J., *Joseph's dream: Joseph Chamberlain and Birmingham's improvement* (Birmingham, 1978)

Upton, C., *A History of Birmingham* (Chichester, 1993)

Vince, C.A., *History of the Corporation of Birmingham* (Birmingham, 1902)

Developing Birmingham 1889 to 1989, 100 years of City Planning (Birmingham, 1989)

Coventry

Demidowicz, G., (ed.), *Coventry's first Cathedral* (Stamford, 1994)

Fox, L., *Coventry's heritage: an introduction to the history of the city* (Coventry, 1947)

Gooder, E., *Coventry's town wall* (Coventry, 1971)

Harris, M.D., *The story of Coventry* (London, 1911)

Lancaster, J.C., *Atlas of Historic towns II: Coventry* (London, 1974)

Phythian-Adams, C., *Desolation of a city: Coventry and the urban crisis of the late Middle Ages* (Cambridge, 1980)

Poole, B., *Coventry, its history and antiquities* (London, 1870)

Richardson, K., *Twentieth century Coventry* (London, 1972)

Rylatt, M., *City of Coventry, archaeology and development* (Coventry, 1977)

Sharp, R., *History and antiquities of the city of Coventry* (London, 1871)

Smith, F., *Coventry, six hundred years of municipal life* (Coventry, 1945)

Index

Brown, Lancelot (Capability), 82, 83, 93
Bubbenhall, 86
Budbrooke, 27, 78
Bulkington, 104
burh, 33, 40
burnt mound, 24
Burton Dassett, 47, 56, 69, 70
Burton Hastings, 24
Butler's Marston, 39

Cadbury family, 91, 132
Calthorpe family, 126
Cawston-on-Dunsmore, 34, 66
cement making, 104
Cestersover, 69
Chad, Saint, 31
Chadshunt, 32
Chamberlain, Joseph, 91, 128-9
chantry chapels, 47, 72
Charlecote, 69, 70, 73, 76, 83, 91, 93
Cherington, 47, 70
Chester, Bishop of, 36, 60
Chester, Earl of, 60, 61
Chesterton, 26, 27, 57, 67, 69, 71, 78, 93
Chilvers Coten, 65
cholera, 120
Churchover, 30, 86, 93
Cistercians, 49, 66
Civil War, 18, 77-80
Clinton, Geoffrey de, 50, 51, 58
Clopton, Sir Hugh, 94
coaching, 96-9, 110, 118
coal-mining, 19, 28, 65, 101-3
coal-transport, 98-100
Cole, river, 91, 32
Coleshill, 28, 31, 38, 39, 44, 77, 87, 91, 95, 97, 113, 116, 130
Colmore family, 122
Combrook, 93
Compton Scorpion, 69
Compton Verney, 67, 82, 83, 93
Compton Wynyates, 20, 70, 73, 75, 77, 80, 81, 93
Coombe Abbey, 49, 66, 73, 81, 83, 90
Copston, 34
Corbucion, William de, 41
Cotswolds, 17, 18, 20, 21, 25, 27, 28, 47, 86, 89, 109
cottage gardens, 43, 53, 55
Coughton Court, 54, 73, 74, 76, 78, 80, 134
Coundon, 32
County of West Midlands, 17, 130

Coutances, Bishop of, 36
Coventry: 17, 20, 21, 31, 37, 40, 43, 46, 47, 49, 50, 54, 55, 59-64, 67, 72, 76, 77, 95, 97, 99, 103, 105, 109, 110, 112, 114, 115, 116, 117, 118, 119, 130, 134; Canal, 99, 103; Diocese, 49, 59; Priory, 48, 58, 59
Craven, Earl of, 81, 90
cursus, 22

Danes, 33, 34, 35, 49
deserted settlements, 66-71
Dissolution of the Monasteries, 46, 49, 72-3, 76, 84
Domesday Book, 32, 35-41
Dordon, 101
Dudley, Robert, Earl of Leicester, 52, 73, 76
Dugdale family, 15, 78, 91, 103
Dunchurch, 95
Dunsmore, 20, 78

East Warwickshire coalfield, 19, 99, 101-3, 113
Edgbaston, 76, 83, 84, 120, 126
Edge Hill, 18, 20, 25, 32, 78-80, 87, 96
Editha, Saint, 49
Elan Valley, 131
Eliot, George, 18
Elmdon, 87, 120, 134
Emscote, 30
enclosure, 69-71, 84-8
Erdington, 125, 127
Ettington, 23, 43, 76, 91
Evesham, battle of, 51
Exhall, 32, 104

fallow, 42
farming systems, 25, 36, 44, 69-71
Farnborough Hall, 81
Fazeley, 104
Feldon, 18, 24, 36, 37, 38, 44, 45, 46, 66, 69, 85, 86, 88, 96, 113
Fenny Compton, 28
Ferrers family, 54
Fillongley, 24
fish ponds, 53, 54, 58, 70, 71
Foleshill, 101, 104
Fosse Way, 18, 26, 29, 30, 40, 41, 58
Fox, George, 76
friars, 50, 55, 61, 62, 72
Fulbrook, 67, 70

Gaunt, John of, 52
Gaydon, 45, 76
Godiva, Lady, 40, 48, 59